UNBROKEN…

I Am Still Standing

Meshia M. Bean

Copyright © 2016 by Meshia M. Bean

All rights reserved. No part of this publication may be reproduced, distributed, or transmitted without the express consent of the author.

Creative Direction: Meshia M. Bean, and Tamiko Lowry-Pugh
Written by Meshia M. Bean
Edited by Bernadine C. Taylor
Cover Photo by Joshua T. Binyard

Printed and bound in the United States of America

First edition – November 2016

ISBN-978-1539733096

DEDICATION

This book is dedicated to all of the young children and adults who have been or are still being violated by a predator. For the ones that I know of personally that have been and still are dealing with this issue, thank you for allowing me to be your voice. This book is for you. There is still hope. Don't EVER give up!

Find a place inside where there's joy, and the joy will burn out the pain.
~Joseph Campbell

ACKNOWLEDGEMENTS

First and foremost I give thanks to my Heavenly Father Jesus Christ for giving me the strength to overcome my fears.

To my loving, wonderful, and handsome son Joshua. They say that dreams do come true. You know Mommy loves you with all of my heart and soul. Thank you for your patience and much-needed support!

To my beautiful Mother, Gwendolynn. Although you are not here in the flesh, I know that you are here in spirit. Thank you so much for sharing the love you have in Jesus. Thank you for making me the strong and independent woman that I am today. I love and miss you so much.

To my wonderful family. My Step-Father Sterling, my two brothers Demetrius and Sterling Jr, and to my lovely Sister-in-law Tanesha. Thank you for all of your love and support.

To my wonderful friends. There are too many to name. You know who you are. Thank you so much for all of your love and putting up with my craziness. I love you all very much!

To Silas Bank Jr. You came in my life at the right moment and the perfect time. Thank you for Pastoring and helping me to grow spiritually. I love you so much.

There are two great days in a person's life - the day we are born, and the day we discover why.
~William Barclay

TABLE OF CONTENTS

Foreword………………………………………………9

Preface…………………………………………………11

Prologue………………………………………………15

Chapter 1: The Beginning……………………………19

Chapter 2: It's Not My Fault...………………………27

Chapter 3: Just a Little Girl…………………………39

Chapter 4: Here We Go Again………………………49

Chapter 5: Still Exposed……………………………61

Chapter 6: I'm Going Back to Cali…………………71

Chapter 7: A Baby Having a Baby…………………79

Chapter 8: Moving to Hotlanta……………………93

Chapter 9: All These Black People………………103

Chapter 10: My Queen……………………………111

Chapter 11: The Monster…………………………119

Chapter 12: I Am Still Standing...………………131

UNBROKEN

MERRIAM-WEBSTER DEFINES UNBROKEN AS
Not damaged or broken, not interrupted, whole, intact.

FOREWORD
By Joshua T. Binyard

When life gets confusing the first person I talk to is my mother, Meshia Bean. She is non-judgmental, trusting, and honest. Her smile is infectious, and her charm is extraordinary. She moves through the world in this majestic way that she doesn't even realize. She is a prominent being in every one of her friend's lives. She is always caring, giving those who need it help, and advice. A true matriarch not even in her prime. I couldn't be happier or more proud of this woman who has given birth to me and raised me. I have watched her plant positive seeds of influence in children and man alike, helping them become better versions of themselves. She has only disciplined me physically twice out my whole life. Her methods of non-violence have guided me and taught me respect and have been way more effective than anyone can ever imagine. My mom is my hero, and just like she has and is still continuing to help me on my journey, I will always help her in any way I can.

"I can do all things through Christ who strengthens me."
Philippians 4:13

PREFACE

My motivation for writing this book is based on my personal life experiences of survivorship. Being molested, and violated by men throughout my life. Taking care of a disabled loved one, and being diagnosed with Multiple Sclerosis has been challenging but through it all… God has kept me.

This book, my real life story is for girls, boys, and most importantly for parents to pay attention and not be afraid to speak up and speak out for your child if you feel he or she is being threatened, hurt, harmed or acting strange around a particular person. It is ok to ask questions. Use your basic instinct! As parents, it is our responsibility to teach our children what we believe to be right. Otherwise, the streets will teach them the wrong thing. Be aware of who you let keep your children. Keep them safe, because they are our future.

For the families who are taking care of a loved one that is bedridden and cannot talk, move, or take care of themselves, make sure you love them and stick by their side until the end. They need your love and support to make it through.

Being diagnosed with Multiple Sclerosis was not easy. I call it "*The Monster*." Although I have to deal with this monster on a daily basis, I can wholeheartedly say… I may have MS, but MS doesn't have me!

I have been battling with writing this story for ten years. My son Joshua convinced me to write. He said *"Go ahead, Mom. Why not do it, what do you have to lose?"*

I'm forty-four years old, Gosh I've been through a lot!

The grass withers and the flowers fall,
but the word of our God endures forever.
Isaiah 40:8

PROLOGUE

It was the year 1978 when all hell broke loose. I went downstairs in the mice infested basement. The entire house had mice running all around. You could hear them in the walls. Especially at night. I had been down there many times before, even though it was the place where the grown-ups hung out. I was looking for my Mother because it was Halloween and I was going to be a princess, and we were going to make some Carmel apples and hand out some candy to the other kids. But I just really wanted to start eating some right then. There was an extra bedroom down in the basement that my Mother and her boyfriend stayed.

As soon as you walk downstairs, there was a bar set up right at the end of the staircase with all kinds of liquor that was stored on it. It had different color lights flashing from it like it was Christmas time. The television was on once I passed the stairs. The lighting in the basement wasn't that bright down there, and the other lights were not on. There was living room furniture, a stereo, two end coffee tables, and a four seated card table.

As I walked further into the basement, I heard Cunningham's voice. He asked me *"what was I doing down here?"* It startled me a little since I didn't notice him at first. When I looked his way, he was laying back on the couch, with his dusty blue jeans, dingy white t- shirt and a red baseball cap on his head. He had a beer in one hand and the other hand, he had resting on a huge black gun. I said to him, *"I'm looking for my Mommy,"* But for some reason, I was a little frightened of him this time. I guess because I had never seen a gun before or maybe because the way he spoke to me. Then Cunningham said, "*She's in her room…you can go knock on the door.*" He was looking at me strangely this time, so I ran past him and knocked on the door, but nobody answered. I knocked again, "*Mom are you in there?*" hoping she would say come in. But still no answer. Then he said "*My mistake, I thought she was in there*" as he chuckled under his breath.

As I quickly turned around and started to walk back towards the stairs, he sat up from the couch so fast, reached out and grabbed me by my arm very hard, "*Come here and give your Grandaddy a hug and a kiss.*" He picked me up and made me sit on his lap. Making me move my hips back and forth and grind on his crotch. I sat on his lap before, but not like this. I froze, and I believe I stopped breathing. The next thing I knew, he threw me on my back onto the couch.

The Lord is Strong; Do not Fear
My flesh and my heart fail, but God is the strength of my heart and my portion forever.
Psalms – 73:26

CHAPTER 1
The Beginning

My parents were married right out of high school. From that marriage a beautiful high yellow baby girl was born on August 13, 1972, at 7:37 a.m. on a Sunday in sunny California. But not on a *Friday the thirteenth,* so that makes me a blessed child I always said.

Everybody thought I was a boy as a newborn with blonde hair. I ended up developing freckles later on in my life; which I did not like them until I matured. I remember my Mother telling me that when she was three months pregnant with me in a gymnastics class in high school that she was on the parallel bar had come in 3rd place. That's why I am so crazy at times. To this day, I am very much a daredevil.

My Mother used to say *"I would read to you while you were in my belly and play classical music."* I asked her *what did I do, or did I respond.* She said, *"You moved around kicking a lot, so I thought you were being stimulated in the right way, but I was wrong!"* She would laugh every time she told that story. I didn't think it was funny at all since afterward she would add, *"you still came out dumb."* At first, it would hurt my feelings, but I later overcame that.

My Mother was a beautiful brown skinned lady with a big smile, big eyes, and a big butt like her Mama. My Mother tried to give my Father a few chances to get his act together and provide a better life for our family. But she soon realized that my Father was a *Mama's boy*. From what my Mother told me…is that he couldn't keep a job long enough to pay the bills, and always called on my Madea for help. We ended up moving in with my Madea for a little while.

So one day my Mother could not take it anymore, and decided the best choice was to pack her and I up and move to Denver Colorado.

I always was told that my name "*Meshia*" means: a girl usually of mystery, very unique. Often known for having superior intellect. Reserved, with a quiet confidence and pure of heart. The name is of Persian origin.

It was always one of my dreams to follow in my Mom's footsteps to become an RN, a *Registered Nurse*. I don't know why she picked that field of work. I attended school to become a Phlebotomist instead. My Mother was happy that I was doing something in the medical field. Anything to allow me to live out my dreams. But when I gave birth to my son, I had to take him to an *in home* daycare. I never knew they even existed. When my provider was closing her in home daycare, I decided to start my own. I talked it over with my husband, and he agreed. So that is what I ended up doing for many years. My husband and I were a team on this!

I didn't play when it came to the children learning. I wasn't just a babysitter. I was a teacher. I raised numerous honor roll students. Everybody knows that teaching is my passion. "*The children are our future.*" I still keep in contact with many of the parents and the children.

To this day, I still don't mind helping others, like cooking and cleaning for my loved ones and my older neighbors. I still babysit from time to time *for free*, and I love it. I am such a nurturer.

I can remember my life starting back to the age of four years old. There were times when I had to watch myself at that age while my Mother had to work or attend school. She would have my food and my drinks already prepared in the fridge. I was instructed not to answer the door. She never mentioned a house phone at the time, so I am assuming we didn't have one. She couldn't pay a babysitter, either, at that time. So I would sit up in the upstairs window, yell outside to other kids, "*hey come and talk to me.*" I remember staying home by myself a quite a bit.

When my Mother was able to make enough money to pay for daycare, she would leave me with a neighbor named *Trisha*. A large white lady, that always wore this dirty robe. She had some pets, but not any kids. Ms. Trisha kept her apartment so nasty and of course it smelled awful. Me personally… I would not have left my child with her. But what choice did my Mother have? My Mom didn't have any other option. I wasn't allowed to do anything at Ms. Trish's house. If I attempted to sit on her furniture, she would get loud, "*Oh no! No kids sitting on the furniture because you will get it dirty!*" But it was already dirty. She handed me a blanket, "*you can sit on this!*" But the pets could flop all over the furniture and shed their hair everywhere. When she fixed my food one day, it had pet hair in it, so I didn't eat it. She didn't really talk to me that much after that.

On two separate occasions, she had a man come by her apartment. She said that he was her brother. As they went into her bedroom, I was told not to bother her and that she would be right out. She told me to sit down and watch cartoons. I was patiently sitting on the floor while the animals were laying all over the furniture! I don't know how long they were in her bedroom, but every now and then I would hear someone knocking on the walls, and the bed making squeaking sounds, and I heard moaning noises. Now that I am older, I know that they were *having sex*.

As soon as she went into the room and closed the door, though, the cats started jumping around from one couch to the other. I thought it was cute until one of the cats scratched my right hand. I cried out, "*Ouch!*" And I set my butt back down on that blanket. My hand became very red and was throbbing real bad.

When her "*so called*" brother come out of the bedroom, he was fixing his belt on his pants and Ms. Trisha, with her nasty self, had a big smile on her face. Her hair was all over her head. She let the man out and locked the door. She turned and looked at me, with her face all twisted, like *I* did something to her. I told her the black cat scratched my hand. She angrily pointed her finger in my face and touched my nose, "*If you hadn't been messing with the cat... he would not have scratched your hand!*" Then I asked her, "*When is my Mommy coming to pick me up?*" She just ignored me, "*I want you to go take a nap. I am not going to sit here, and have you staring at me. Lay down and close your little eyes.*" I laid down on the cover that she gave me, turned my head the other way and started crying quietly to myself, hoping my Mother would hurry up and come to get me.

I was so nervous that I was afraid to ask her can I go to the bathroom to *pee*! She didn't even ask me if I was cold. That heifer! There was a knock on the door. I sat up so fast, hoping it was my

Mom. Ms. Trisha opened the front door, and both of them said hello to each other at same time. Before she could say *"Your Mom is here,"* I was already running towards the door yelling *"Mommy!"* I was jumping up and down, *"Let's go home now Mom!"* Ms. Trisha tried to give me a hug, but I just looked at her with disgust and yanked away. You know how kids do; *"my Mother is her, so now!"* I mused silently.

My Mother picked me up to give me a kiss, and a hug, *"What the hell is wrong with you?"* And told me to calm down. As we were walking home, she asked, how my day was, and *"Did Ms. Trisha fed you?"* I said, *"No, I didn't eat."* I told her there was animal hair in the food. Although my Mother talked to Ms. Trisha once before about that, she then asked, *"What did you two do today?"* So I rapidly told her, *"Ms. Trisha's brother came by, and they went into her bedroom, and she told me not to bother her, and she closed the door and left me with all of her animals and that the black cat scratched my hand! And she pointed her finger in my face touching my nose. And when that man had left she made me go take a nap because I didn't want to eat."*

You know you ask a child one question, and they will tell you everything. I started crying, "I don't want to go back to Ms. Trisha's house anymore." So for the next couple of weeks, my Mother let me stay home by myself. She felt I was better off *watching myself*. That's when I had to start being mature. There was nothing around to distract me and by *the grace of God... He watched over me at that young age*.

My Mother had met this man; his name was Wilbur. He started to hang around my Mom a lot. From what I remember he was a very light skinned man with freckles also and a red afro. He thought he was cool a brother. He would wear these beige bell bottom pants, these crazy looking colored shirts with a large collar, and shoes that had heels on them. He was the neighborhood drug dealer that always tried to get my Mom to go out with him.

We started hanging out at his apartment. He had a sister, named *"Vicki."* I was told to call her *"Aunt Vicki."* She was mixed with black and Indian. I thought she was a beautiful lady with long black straight hair that she would let me play in. I would sometimes wish I had hair like hers so I could flip it from side to side. My Mother trusted this woman to watch me. She even had a daughter that was my age, so I had a friend to play with. Her name was Lisa, and we grew up together over the years.

She was a high yellow girl like me with a lot of thick hair, and she had a smart mouth. She always talked back to her Mother and never got in trouble for it. One day, we were in my Moms yellow two-door Mercedes-Benz playing like we were driving, when Lisa pulled the lever down in reverse and the car started rolling down the street backwards, and all I know is that my Mother was running after the car and yelling for us to step on the break, and this chick was turning the steering wheel from right to left, like she was actually driving. I didn't know what my Mother was talking about… *some brakes*. By the grace of God, my Mom was able to jump in the driver's side and stopped the car before we caused an accident. We both got our butts beat for that… but it didn't stop us from getting in trouble.

Another time I ended up following Lisa again. Our Moms left us home with Wilbur, and we had made a tent in the front yard with some blankets we took from inside the house, and a few lawn chairs. She had some cigarettes and matches that she had taken from her Mother's purse. She lit one up, pulled it and blew out some smoke then she passed it to me, and I didn't know what to do, so I did what Lisa did. I put the cigarette to my mouth and pulled it, and I guess I swallowed the smoke because I started choking real bad, my eyes were watering and started burning real bad. Lisa said to me, "*You do it like this!*" She told me that I had to hold it between her two fingers and was smoking it like a grown woman. She lit another one, but this time our man made tent caught on fire. A neighbor came outside because she had seen some smoke coming from the blanket, snatched the blanket and threw whatever she had in her cup on the fire, yelling at us while she ran to get Wilbur. We had to wait inside the apartment for our Mother's to get back. I didn't like to be inside there because he always had a lot of people in there smoking weed and drinking, but mainly there was this large blue and red velvet crush picture of the devil! With horns and the eyes seemed always to move and follow me. I would run by it all the time. I was five going on six years old, and at that time, that picture always scared the shit out of me. I would just stare at it for a long time waiting for the right moment to run past it. I still see that image to this day and always wondered why someone would have a picture of a devil hanging on their wall.

When our Mother's arrived home and were told what we did… do you know they made us sit in front of them and show them how we were smoking? I was crying and choking saying; *I will never smoke again,* and Lisa just was smoking the cigarette *like a pro*. But things didn't last long with my Mother and Wilbur. I noticed one day, he was pushing and grabbing at my Mom, then out of nowhere, he balled his hand up, and punched my Mom in her face, all because he was jealous of all of the attention she was getting from a lot of other men. My Mother tried to fight him back but she was a small woman, and her hits didn't even make him flinch. I saw her cry, but not out of any fear of him; she was crying because she was pissed off that he had hit her in front of her little girl. At least I know where I get my feistiness come from… *my Mother and Grandmother*.

But with things getting worse, my Mother had no choice but to send me to my Father in California for a few months. That was the first and only time I had seen her get hit by any other man.

CHAPTER 2
It's Not My Fault

"*I had to grow up real fast.*" My Mother had a boyfriend, and with the both of them working they struggled together at times, *but* we never went hungry. With him being new in my life, I felt some type of way. I remember meeting him when I was six years old; I had just come from Los Angeles from visiting my Dad for the summer.

My Mother had her new boyfriend pick me up from the airport. He was a tall, dark-skinned man with an afro, mustache, slim build. A handsome man. He didn't look like the last one, but he dressed like him. That was the style in the 1970's.

He came and picked me up in his two-tone dark and light blue van that had dolphins on the sides (that his ex-wife had put sugar in the gas tank; I overheard my Mom telling a girlfriend *that* story). He said, "*Hi,*" and proceeded to tell me his name was "*Tommy*" and that he was my new Daddy, *smiling while he said that*. I just looked at him, wondering what was going on. I was like… *I hope he is nothing like her last boyfriend because I will help fight this time*. When we pulled up to the house, and I saw my Mother standing outside on the porch, I was smiling so big, happy to see my Mommy. *I love her so much*! I then saw her stomach. It was so round. My Mother was pregnant with my brother, *Jr*. I don't recall being around a pregnant woman before. I ran up and put both of my hands on her stomach. I was excited because my cousins in Los Angeles had siblings. She kissed me and said *"Hey big sister."* So they both lived with my Granny her name was Betsy Mae, a short dark skinned woman, with a gold tooth in her mouth. She had a big butt and loved her blonde hair and her drunken husband whose name was *Cunningham*. I was greeted with open arms.

Soon, my first-grade year was about to start, and I was told that I had to walk to school all by myself because everybody had to go to work in the mornings and that 'I know how to take care of myself' because I had done it many times before. My Mother put her hand on my jaw to make me look at her, "Do not stop and talk to any strangers, just keep walking, and I mean do not stop for no one and do not tell the teacher that you walked by yourself." She gave me a door key that was on a shoe string to put around my neck, and said, "I am serious… are you listening to me?" I said, "Yes Mommy, I am listening." I remember feeling my heart beating thinking I have to lock the door with a key and hope that I would not lose the key. We had done a practice run before school had started.

My Mother told me when to leave for school, *after the seven o'clock news went off*, and showed me how to lock the front door. The good thing is *that* I knew how *to tell time*. I had to grow up real fast. My Granny told me that I had to learn how to cook if I wanted to eat, so she would have me help her in the kitchen. I made bacon and eggs for breakfast, sandwiches for lunch and she showed me how to fry chicken, peel potatoes for dinner, and how to wash dishes and if I broke a dish she would hit me with her key chain. You know the one you made with the braided different color plastic rope. My Step Grandad would come in the kitchen and say to me *"What's for dinner little lady?"* and rub my back, *"You're going to make a good housewife one day"* then give me a kiss on my forehead. I did *feel* like a little lady from all the grown things that I had to do.

My Granny would say, *"Not if she cooks like her damn Mama... chicken still have the feathers all on it, and look like they're about to jump out the grease and fly away."*

One day, *Cunningham,* that's what everyone called my Step Grandad (and now that I'm older and know better, this dirty old man was making his move on me), bought me a baby doll with this silky blonde hair, blue eyes, and she had on this crushed velvet red dress and some candy. He would always kiss my hand and tell me how pretty I looked. I don't recall ever being told or talked to about child molesting back then. He always asked my Mom could he take me to school the days he was off or he would let me help him in the yard, or I would be the errand girl (getting a beer and cups of ice for his friends when he had company). He always wanted me to sit on his lap, and he would have me bouncing and wiggle around on his lap too. It was fun to me at that time. I thought he loved me... I guess like a Grandfather should have. *Nobody didn't see anything wrong with this picture*! Never let a little girl sit in the middle of a man's lap. Have them sit next to them.

My Mom always dressed me in pretty clothes. One time I had on a black and white dress with black poke-a-dots all over it with white ruffled socks. When Cunningham saw me, he acted so surprise. He never called me a little girl. He would always say *"my little lady."* I was told that I was going to have a house guest. My cousin Tina was my Uncle's stepdaughter visiting from the Carolina's. That was my first time meeting her. We were the same age so again; I had someone to play with and help me with some of the responsibilities around the house. I didn't accept the idea that I had to share my room with her. One morning my cousin and I woke up and the bed was wet. I knew I didn't pee in the bed, so I told her she had to tell Granny what she did. But she didn't and when my Granny came in the room to have us change the sheets, she noticed that the bed was wet, and yelled for use to *come here* and asked, "*Who pee'd in her got-damn bed?*" And of course, we both said *not me*! But for some reason, Grandmother didn't believe me. So my Granny told me she was going to *beat my little ass*!

I kept saying, "*But Granny I didn't pee in your bed... I didn't pee in your bed.*" crying this time. My Granny was quick to hit somebody. It's like she got off on that. I was asking for my Mommy by this time and my Granny said she is not here to save you and *your ass is mine*! At that point, Cunningham offered to spank me himself. I was so scared because I didn't care who was going to do it. I just didn't want a spanking! So I started crying... I mean crying and screaming loud like I was about to die. My cousin was just standing there looking at me with her wide eyes. I'm looking at her thinking, "*I am going to get you heifer!*" Cunningham grabbed my hand, and I followed him into my bedroom. He said, "*be quiet... this is what I want you to do, I am going to hit the bed with my belt, and I want you to holler, and cry like I'm hitting you.*" So he took his black belt from his pants, hit the bed four times and each time I had to act like I was really getting hit but I put my hand over my mouth because I was laughing inside. He said for me to stay in my room for a while so it would like I cried myself to sleep. But still, nobody came in and checked on me. I thought that was so cool. He was my Grandaddy and my best friend (*but that was just to get me to like and trust him*)!

He would let me drink coffee and even let me take a few swigs of BEER! But my Mother knew he would let me drink coffee sometimes but she told him no more because it will "*stunt my growth*" but he still gave it to me anyway. I would ride to the store with him to get coffee, donuts and a Sunday paper on Sunday mornings to bring back to my Mom and Grandmother. My Grandmother had a lovely looking home from the outside. The house was gray and red. During Christmas time she would go all out with all kinds of decorations like a Santa Claus with his slide, Rudolph the reindeer on top of the roof and Mary and baby Jesus and the three wise men, and even a snowman in the front yard. She did that for many years.

When you come in the front gate, you walk up the stairs to a large front porch that my cousin and I were allowed to camp out on sometimes with a television and radio. And when you come in the front door, there was a burgundy staircase going upstairs and the walls had a wood panel with three nice size bedrooms. One bathroom, that was painted a throw up green color even the bathtub and the toilet were that color also and down stairs to the first room on your left was a living room. Down the hallway, you walk straight into the kitchen with the largest silver refrigerator I have ever seen, and there was second room on the left of you which was the dining room with a piano in there. Come to find out later, I actually learned that was my Mother's piano that I played on from time to time. I wish I had learned how to play the piano, then *the* door that led to the basement.

As I walked further into the basement, I heard Cunningham's voice. He asked me "*what was I doing down here?*" It startled me a little since I didn't notice him at first. When I looked his way, he was laying back on the couch, with his dusty blue jeans, dingy white t- shirt and a red baseball cap on his head. He had a beer in one hand and the other hand, he had resting on a huge black gun. I said to him, *"I'm looking for my Mommy,"* But for some reason, I was a little frightened of him this time. I guess because I had never seen a gun before or maybe because the way he spoke to me. Then Cunningham said, *"She's in her room...you can go knock on the door."* He was looking at me strangely this time, so I ran past him and knocked on the door, but nobody answered. I knocked again, *"Mom are you in there?"* hoping she would say come in. But still no answer. Then he said *"My mistake, I thought she was in there"* as he chuckled under his breath.

As I quickly turned around and started to walk back towards the stairs, he sat up from the couch so fast, reached out and grabbed me by my arm very hard, *"Come here and give your Grandaddy a hug and a kiss."* He picked me up and made me sit on his lap. Making me move my hips back and forth and grind on his crotch. I sat on his lap before, but not like this. I froze, and I believe I stopped breathing. The next thing I knew, he threw me on my back onto the couch.

Cunningham climbed on top of me, pulling my panties off and trying to put this black snake looking thing between my legs. I remember feeling this horrible pain trying to enter into my vagina. I was only six years old. I was so scared; I didn't know what was going on. All I could do is *think is my Grandfather, my friend was on top of me.* He was forcing his grown man penis, of what he could, inside of me. I was crying and trying to push his big body off of my little girl's body. He was trying to soothe me by rubbing my hair, and he kept kissing me on my face with his stinking beer breath. He was telling me to *relax, to be still* and said that I would eventually like this and that he is showing me how to be a woman. *But I am just a little girl*!

It was hurting so damn bad. It felt like I was being split in half. I was looking up at him begging him to stop. I was hitting him on his head and his arms with both of my fist, and saying *"you're hurting me."* I could hardly breathe. His body was suffocating me. I blacked out… I guess. I remember him saying to me to keep my mouth shut and If I said anything that he would kill my Mother and he pointed at the gun he had laying on the brown coffee table. He got up off of me and wiped this wet stuff off from between my legs. I noticed I was bleeding from my vaginal area from what I remember. I guess he threw my panties away because my Mom didn't say anything about seeing any blood or seeing my panties.

Consider it pure joy, whenever you face trials of many kinds, because that the testing of your faith develops perseverance.
- James 1:2

A child molester- is an older child or adult who touches a child for her or his sexual gratification.

Child Molestation- Is the act of sexually touching a child of the age 13yrs or younger.

How Can We Spot a Child Molester?
By Katherine Ramsland Ph.D.

Stereotypes of sexual predators can be misleading. It is nearly impossible to prospectively determine who a sexual predator might be. Someone who looks 'creepy' is no more an offender then a respectable person, as well, just because someone seems respectable does not eliminate him (or her) as a child molester.

Accurate prediction based on traits, appearance, still remains outside of reach. There is a book called "Inside the Minds of Sexual Predators," with Patrick Grain.

Pedophiles are often placed into one of four categories. Pedophiles are often placed into one of four categories. The first is the *mysoped*. These offenders are interested in molesting and sexually abusing children because they want to physically harm them.

A second type is the *regressed child offender*. This individual generally has relations with adults but offends against a child because of a stressful event in the offender's life that makes him seek someone he can control.

The *fixated child offender* is stuck at an early stage of psychosexual development. He has little to no activity with people his own age and is often uncomfortable around adults. He loves children and does not want to hurt them, so he rationalizes that abuse is actually affection.

Finally, the ***naïve*** <u>pedophile</u> is the individual who, for all intents and purposes, has no sense of right and wrong. The offender is often mentally retarded or unstable and does not comprehend the rules of normal society.

When researchers Reuben Lang and Roy Frenzel interviewed 52 incest and 50 pedophilic offenders, they found that the average age of child molesters is thirty-four. Updated stats indicate that 25% are over 40. A typical modus operandi is to befriend the <u>parents</u> and offer to babysit the victims. They are attracted to situations in which children are easily attainable, and might even set them up. They gradually insert themselves into the victims' lives.

Once they achieve success, the most common initial contact is "accidental" touching or cuddling. This allows the offender to be close to a child without him or her suspecting that anything out of the ordinary is occurring. If caught, it's easy to say it's a misunderstanding. Like in my situation, my pedophile used coercion and frightened me into compliance with threats against my Mother. He also bribed me to ensure silence to gain consent. He misrepresents normal moral standards to seduce me gradually into believing that nothing bad is happening to me.

"Bad things do happen how I respond to them defines my character and the quality of my life. I can choose to sit in perpetual sadness, immobilized by gravity of my loss, or I can choose to rise from the pain and treasure the most precious gift I have – life itself."

-Walter Anderson

CHAPTER 3
Just a Little Girl

My Mother didn't know what just happened to me. I was in so much pain. No one even noticed that something was wrong with me or if I was acting difficult… *How would they know if nobody wasn't paying any attention to me in the first place*? So some time passed by… I am not sure how long before Cunningham was back at it again.

My Mom and Granny told my cousin Tina and me to go down in the basement because they had to go to the store for some groceries; that they would be back later and that *Cunningham* was asleep on the couch, and for us '*not to bother him.*' Man, when she said that, my heart started beating so *damn* fast! I did not want to go down there again; especially if he was going to be down there. When we went down to the basement my, Step-Grandfather was sitting on the couch watching the television. When he saw us, he said, "*Come here and sit with me, I am watching the Denver Bronco's I know Meshia likes football.*" He would ask me what team was *going to win* so that he would bet me like fifty cents. I was a little scared, but I wasn't alone this time, so I felt '*okay.*' We played a little bit with our toys, then Tina laid her butt down on the floor and fell asleep. I tried to wake her up but that was '*no use,*' and it started again. He told me to '*come here,'* and there was that *black gun* again, and some candy and some money next to him. He told me to '*get on my knees.*' I started crying and said, '*NO!*' He grabbed me by the back of my neck and made me crawl closer to him. He unbuttoned his jeans, pulled out his penis and told me to *"stick my tongue out* and *put it on his penis* and *lick it."* He then told me to put it in *"my mouth and suck on it like a popsicle"* and *"you better not scrape me with your teeth, or I will slap you across your face."* He was already choking me with his hand. I was so scared; I was shaking so bad, choking and crying. That was my first time giving 'head.' I know that sounds crazy for me to be saying this now because I joke around and, say, *"I've been giving head since I was six years old."* Folks would be like, *"What is this crazy chic talking about?"* That would usually give me the opportunity to explain what I went through as a young child.

It was *1980*; I was eight years old, and we still lived with my Grandmother and *that man*. One night I had to ride with *Cunningham* to go pick up my Granny from work at the hospital, where she worked as a cook in the cafeteria, and on the way, he pulled over and told me that he had to show me something… he pulled out his penis and told me to stroke it up and down… *"Why me? Why did I have to do these kind of things?"* He tried to push my head down towards his crotch, but this time I bit him on his penis, he jumped and yanked me from the back of my hair and pushed my head off of him and called me a *'little bitch!'* And said, *"I should beat your ass for real this time,"* he threatened me again by saying, *"You better not say anything to anyone or I will kill my Mom."* Somehow I knew it was wrong because it didn't feel right and I wasn't going to do that anymore! Cunningham didn't touch me anymore, but he would show me his penis from time to time and taunt, *"You want some?"* I don't remember when and how it all stopped. I assume he knew what he did was wrong or maybe he found another young child. The neighborhood was filled with a lot of kids. I did my best to avoid him as much as possible anyway because I said to myself, '*If this asshole touches me again... I will fight this time,*' but I didn't want to tell anybody because I was afraid that he really would have hurt my Mother.

One summer day, I was at my friend's house playing kickball in their yard. They lived about five houses from me. Dawn and Paula were sisters. They lived on the corner, and right next door to their house was a liquor store and a barbecue joint and a little hole in the wall (*a nightclub*). Now as I look back at the neighborhood, it was a *hoe Stroll*! It was always something going on; *on that corner* from killings, robbery or knife fights. The homes were all very beautiful from the outside but who knew what was going on behind closed doors! *Like behind my closed doors*! My Step Grandfather came over to tell me that my Uncle David was on the phone, he was my Mothers' younger brother. Evidently, my Uncle must have said something to my cousin in conversation about my Step Grandfather. So my cousin, who I thought was sleeping, well, she saw the whole thing... with my having to give oral sex to that pervert and she saw the gun. He was telling me to say that my cousin was '*lying*,' and that '*I didn't know what she was talking about.*' I was running back towards my house trying to get away from him, and he was running behind me, and he kept saying "*tell him you don't know what she is talking about!* So I got on the phone... my Uncle lived in Germany, at that time, he was in the army... I picked up the phone and said, "Hello Uncle?" Cunningham was standing right there looking at me for a few seconds with his eyes wide open, looking nervous. My Uncle said, "*What the hell is your cousin Tina talking about? She told me what your Grandfather had you doing?!?!*" I couldn't tell a story, so I said, "*Yes. It's true.*" I remember saying to him, "*He said *he would kill my Mother so I cannot tell anybody!*" He yelled at me through the phone and told me to '*get my Mom now!*' So, I put the phone down and went down to the basement. My Mom, her boyfriend, Granny and *the pervert* and another couple were playing cards. Listening to blues music. They had some red drinking cups; most likely with alcohol in them and talking shit to each other. My Mother looked up at me and said, '*how can I help you, my child?*' I just yelled out in front of everybody, "*Ma... Uncle is on the phone, and he wants to talk you about Cunningham... that he has been goosing me,*" that's what I called it. She said, "*What?!*" and to say that again… so I repeated it again, "*Cunningham has been goosing me!*" Everything just stopped, and my Mother was in disbelief. Her face turned pale. My Mom turned to my Granny and started yelling at her saying, "*What the hell is Meshia talking about!*" They both started fussing at each other and waving their hands all around. Her boyfriend and Step Grandaddy started yelling also. I didn't understand why anybody didn't call the police! But now I do. In the *'80's*, nobody reported child molesting back then. You know the sad part of it all, my Granny blamed me. She called me a *red devil*, and if I would have stop hanging around him, and my Mother would have stopped dressing me all cute; maybe it would have never happened! All my Step Grandaddy kept saying was, "*I didn't touch that lying little girl, and he kept calling me a liar.*" I do remember I had to stay at a friend's house for a few days until my Mother found us a new place.

My Mother took me to the Doctor's to get me checked out, and we were told sometimes females are born with their hymen already broken. So they could not say whether anything happened to me at that time and what looked like a scar; it had already healed up. They showed me two dolls, a boy doll that had a penis and a girl doll and asked me where I had been touched and to show him where or how was I positioned as well. I am sure this had to be new to this Doctor because nobody didn't report *anything; still*. I believe they gave my Mom a choice so no one would get in trouble. So, the next thing I knew we were moving to an apartment complex right across the street from my elementary school. The one I had to walk to by myself in which we only lived there for a little while. I had some friends that lived there also. I was too young to remember, but I loved my Mother, so when she moved I moved. I could have asked to go to my Dad's, but I didn't.

On a summer day, I decided to put on a cute summer dress and go outside and play with my friends, but who did I see! *William*, my first boyfriend, that's what I called him. He was a tall skinny, real dark skinned boy with a huge afro. His Mom and my Mom were friends also. We use to watch each other along with some other kids when the grown-ups would go out to the clubs. When we saw each other, I don't remember what was said, but I must have said "*I don't have on any panties*," because I remember lifting up my dress. He said, "*Oh!*" And his eyes were huge looking downwards. My Mother saw what I was doing, she jumped up from her lawn chair, dropped her red cup and starting running after me and cussing at me; she was mad as hell! I don't know where she had gotten the belt from, maybe while we were running around the yard, someone handed it to her… I think that's what happened, but she was swinging that belt like crazy, I could not outrun her! Man, she was whipping me in front of everybody!! (The complex always had parties always on the weekends, so it was a lot of spectators). My Mom was hitting me where ever that belt landed, she actually hit me in the face with it, and she even bust my lip with that belt! I was so scared… blood was running down my mouth and onto my clothes. I ran into our apartment, into the wall of the bathroom and hit my head on the toilet; my Mother continued whooping me, even when I climbed onto my bed! I knew I had to cry myself to sleep. Now that I think about it, I was acting out from being touched as a young child.

I remember my Mom cutting the extension cord from an iron, and she beat me for breaking this tall, slender glass case that was filled with candies like the miniature Hershey chocolate. I had to walk around with long sleeves shirts and jeans in the summer to cover up the marks on my arms and my legs but for what, the whole complex already knew and saw what had happened. My Mom would beat me because that's what my Granny did to her, that's all she knew.

One sunny Sunday morning, I woke up still in my dirty clothes from Saturday. My hair was all over my head, and I went into my Mother's bedroom to ask her if I could go to church with the *Westbrook's sisters*? They were two old white ladies that had taken a liking to me. They lived down the block. *I learned early on 'never ask your Mom anything while she is sleeping.'* My Mother said, "*Yes girl*," she was hung over from the night before from one of the apartment complex parties. So I left the house; without washing my face and brushing my teeth, of course, I was only eight years old. I went over to the Westbrook's house. I knocked on their front door, and *Ms. Lilley* opened it and looked at me from head to toe. She was smiling and called out to her sister, *Ms. Mary*, (she was the older one), when she came from the other room, Ms. Mary just looked at me and said, "*Child! You're wearing pants! And your shirt is a little filthy baby and does your Mom know you're going to church with us?*" I said, "*Yes.*" jumping around not caring that I am dirty and that my hair was looking a mess. *I was just a kid*! They didn't know my Mom; only in passing and maybe spoke a few words; waving to each other. So, we all got in their *white 1964 Lincoln* and off we went to their church service. I know I hadn't even eaten anything at all. When we walked in the church; the people were staring at me. They were probably wondering why is this little black child with these white women. All I know is that I was smiling because I was *happy to be there*.

The funny thing is… we sat in the front row, and the church service was being televised! I sat down, but I kept looking back and talking to people behind me, and Ms. Mary had told me twice that I had to sit still and be quiet. Next thing I knew she pinched me! Of course, I hollered, and the Pastor stopped the service and told the sisters that we had to leave. I bet they had to start the service from the beginning. I can laugh at all of this now because… '*I am still standing*!!' We made our way back to the car, and Ms. Lilley said, "*That is why I gave my child up for adoption*" and she went on to say, *she did not have time for this, and I was an untrained child*! They were rushing to get back to their house; they didn't even drop me off at my home. When we arrived at their house, they told me to go home and not to come back over there anymore!

So I was skipping home, and I saw my Auntie Vicki outside sitting with some other ladies, and I yelled out to her "*Hi*" waving my hand *all happy*. But that changed fast. She looked at me *as they say* 'if looks can kill!' She came up to me and started shaking me,

"*Where have you been?! Your Mom has been looking all over for you... you're about to get a whooping!*" She took off her belt and of course I took off running; there was a park attached to the complex. I took off running through that, and so did she! She was running behind me saying, "*I am going to beat your ass!*" I was like, "*What did I do!?! I asked my Mom could I go to church!*" I know we had to run around this little park area at least twice, again, it was connected to the apartment complex. So she couldn't run anymore because she smoked cigarettes and a lot of weed and was out of breath. Finally, I stopped and begged her not to spank me; she said she would let '*my Mom beat my ass.*' She was breathing so hard I don't think she had the energy to hold up that belt to hit me anyway. I had to go to my room and wait for my Mother to come home to beat my ass when she did arrive home; I was asleep. She woke me up. It was already dark outside. She was gone all day... out looking for me and I had been home for a while. She came into my room and asked me '*where I was at*' and that she had been looking all over for me and she didn't know where else to look. "*Mom you said I could go to church with the old sisters,*" and she said, "*Is this what you had on and look at your hair!*" She was hugging me and said she '*loved me*' and told me '*not to ask her any questions while she was sleeping.*' I was still waiting for my spanking, but she didn't give me one! *Thank you, Jesus*! We went to the movies to see '*Godzilla*' instead.

Anyone who does wrong will be repaid for his wrong, and there is no favoritism.
~Colossians 3:25

CHAPTER 4
Here We Go Again

We were moving again. That meant I had to attend another new school and make new friends. '*Man, it seemed like we were moving a few times a year.*' We moved to a quiet neighborhood near a police station. It was a brown brick house with a beautiful backyard. There were trees with lovely white flowers all over the neighborhood. That's when I got my first dog named *Peanut*. He was a brown, golden retriever.

The house had a basement, which is where my room was; it was a small room but big enough for a twin sized bed, and a dresser with a TV on it. I was afraid to sleep down there because it was creepy, dark and dusty and it smelled. It had another room and bathroom that the toilet wouldn't flush that well, so you know what that meant, that our waste wouldn't go down the drain very well. I learned later that the house we were living in was my Moms boyfriend's ex-wife's house. I made a new friend; her name was *Pamela*; she lived across the street from me in a gray and black house. She was an only child, and after all this time, I just found out recently she was adopted. She had a sheepdog named *Buddy*. I would go to church with them a lot. Pam's Mom bought us matching dresses and shoes for church, and we would always go to a restaurant for dinner after church almost every Sunday. We played with each other all the time. There were other kids to play with, but we didn't care for them too much.

I would go to her house early in the mornings, and her Mom would be like, "*little girl, she is still sleeping baby*," but she would still let me in anyway. We would ride our bikes down this dirt road on *39th and Jackson Street* and go over our neighbors *Mr. and Mrs. Timmons* house. He had a camper and would give us sodas to drink, and told me to come inside the *camper* that he had *something he wanted to show me*. I still did not learn my lesson. So one summer morning I went in, and this dirty old man grabbed me so fast, he was breathing all heavy. He smelled like pee. He was feeling on my little breasts and putting his hands down my shorts. I was able to get away from him, but I still didn't tell my Mother. To this day, I wonder why I didn't say anything. I wonder if I *did* would I have gotten in trouble for going in the camper.

I remember he would *rub his crotch* every time we would go over there. I told Pam what he did, and she told her Mom. Her Mother said we could not go back over anymore, but my Mom didn't know what was going on. I had a bad habit of leaving the house without even asking for permission. I remember one night, I was staying the night, and I got sick. I was throwing up, and I even had *the runs*, so I shitted in her Mom's bed! Her Mom wasn't mad at me, but I think that was my last time staying the night.

One day Pam and I decided to become '*blood sister,*' we got something sharp and cut our fingers, put them together and put some string around our two fingers and said '*we are sisters forever.*' And we are still sisters to this day. Thank God our fingers didn't get infected. I remember Pamela and her Mom went out of town, and I had to play with the other kids, one in particular, her name was Yvonne. She was one of eight children. I didn't care for her not one bit; she was a trouble maker, just so *damn* mean! Now I understand why she acted the way she did. It was so much going on at her house. She had a lot of brothers, a Father that was a drunk and her Mom always stayed in the kitchen cooking for all those children. I remember she tried to bully Pam and me at school. She had us eating grass and told us to put our fingers in each other's noses and eat the boogers. She would also try to take my lunch. *Not my food, I didn't play that*!

One day on the school bus, I was sitting in front of Yvonne, and she started messing with my hair. My Mother didn't play when it came to my hair. *She always told me never to let anyone put their hands in my hair*! Yvonne kept messing with my ponytail and pulling it saying '*that my hair was ugly and that I should let her fix it for me.*' The next thing I knew, I turned around in my seat, got up on my knees, reached down to her and started swinging my hands at her head, pulling her hair and calling her a chicken head. I told her never to touch my hair again. After that day, she was trying to be my best friend and even invited me to the movies to see '*Bambi.*' I went and enjoyed myself, and I have never seen her again.

Well, it was about that time for us to move again. My parents left me and my baby brother *Demetrius (Meat);* he was only a few months old, alone in this new house. It had three bedrooms and one bathroom, and the cool thing about this house was that it had a spiral staircase that led up to my parents' room… just big enough to fit a queen-sized bed and a dresser. While my parents were out getting some food for us, there was a knock at the front door. I thought it was my parents. It was dark outside, so I looked through the blinds, and there was a Mexican male with his face pressed up against the window, smiling at me, showing his yellow and brown *messed up* teeth. He must have been watching the house while we were moving in. I closed the blind down so fast; my heart was beating *so fast*, and it felt like it was trying to come through my throat. So, I ran upstairs to my parent's room, with my little brother in my arms. We didn't have a house phone installed yet; so I couldn't call the police. I should not have been home alone anyway and I could get my parents in trouble because I was under age and my brother was a baby. I hid, with my brother, on the floor… next to the bed, hoping that the creepy man would leave. He began to turn the doorknob, and shake the door saying, "*I know your home alone little girl.*" After a few minutes, he left. It seemed like forever until my parents came back home. By the time they did arrive, I had already calmed down, so I told them what happened. My Stepfather went across the street and started yelling and cursing the men out who were sitting outside the complex, and warned them that he would come and start shooting anybody that messed with his family!

As time passed and we got into the groove with the new area. Mom worked in the day time at the hospital, and my Stepdad worked at night. One cold Saturday morning, I was outside with two new friends, *Natalie and Miguel*, they were both Mexican. We were playing with the jump rope, and my Stepdad came outside with my baby brother, *Meat*, he was about ten months old. He asked me to watch him because he had just gotten off of work and he needed to get some rest. He brought out his walker, and I put him in it. I tied the walker to the stair rail with my jump rope as tight as I could, but when little Meat stood up to walk in the Walker, he fell down the steps in his walker and tumbled over. He was face down crying so loud that I ran down the steps behind him before my Stepdad could hear him. But my Stepdad yanked the front door open so fast, came out of the house in his blue robe yelling at me. "*You're supposed to be watching your brother!*" I was watching him and playing at the same time, but I am just a small kid myself. I picked my brother up and noticed that he had busted his nose. My friends looked at each other with their mouths wide open like, '*did this baby just fall down the stairs.*' He was actually bleeding! He took him out of my arms and was mumbling some crap as he went back in the house and slammed the door so hard the windows shook. I know he was mad because my brother had just woke up and he wasn't going to get any sleep *anytime soon*. Still to this day my brother *Meat* still has the scar on his nose. We were just talking about this recently.

So I left with my friends and went to Natalie's house. I didn't tell my Stepdad that I was leaving. Nat lived with her Mother and her younger brother. We still were able to play with some other kids in the neighborhood. Some of the girls didn't like me being friends with Nat. One of them began to pick on me… calling me a *nigger*, pushing me and pulling my hair. She said '*my hair was so hard that it cut her hand.*' The other kids were laughing with her. Nat yelled at her for her to *leave me alone*, but before I knew it, I grabbed a hand full of this chick's straight hair and was trying to pull what I had in my hands out of her head. Now her friends weren't laughing anymore… they were like '*wow.*' By then Nat's Mother came out of her house yelling at us '*to stop,*' and made the other kids leave her yard. *I was ready to beat her ass.* Her Mom didn't ask what happened either; I just remember hearing Olivia Newton-John's Song, "*Let's Get Physical*" coming out of the house, and she told us she needed some things from the corner store. Sometimes I would eat over there with her family. Her Mother was protective of us going to the store. She told us to be careful and then said something in Spanish to Nat. We were walking and playing the game. *'don't step on the crack 'cause you will break your Mama's back'* and all of sudden Nat told me that we had to switch coats and hats and she said to stuff my hair in the hat because she said she saw her Dad following us. *Talk about being scared*. She had told me she also was molested by her Father and he didn't know where her family lived. I didn't tell her what happened to me.

Later that year, we moved *again* to another house in a new neighborhood. It was a nice area; but directly across the street was a three story, old creepy, burned up house that I had to look at every day. This time, I had a beautiful room, with a new bedroom set. My walls were yellow, and my covers were pink. I had a closet full of brand new clothes and shoes. I believe it was tax time. My Mother brought me this pretty pink and white diary with a silver key to lock it and a *Children's Bible.* For some reason, the book of *Matthew's* was my favorite book. I had to attend another school and make new friends again... When the kids heard about where I lived, they told me that a family had been murdered in there and that they were burned up in the house.

One day, a boy in my class named *Christopher*, told me a scary tale about the old house. There was this little white girl who had had a dog. Every time she would put her hand down towards the floor, the dog would lick her hand, to let her know everything was safe. So, she put her hand down, and he licked her hand. She knew it was okay to get out of her bed. The little girl went downstairs to see if her Mom had made breakfast. When she went into the kitchen, she saw her Mother dead on the floor, with blood coming from her head.

She then went into the living room and saw her two brothers on the couch with blood coming from their heads also. So she ran back upstairs and closed her bedroom door, jumped on her bed and pulled the covers up to her neck. She put her hand down so her dog could lick her hand. The dog licked her hand, well at least she thought it was her dog! When she looked up at the door, she saw a note with the dog's tongue stuck to it. The note said, *"Dogs are not the only thing that can lick."* I was so scared to walk by that house; I would have nightmares all the time about it. Kids can be so mean.

One of my friends was named *Maria*. I would walk a long way to visit her I went to a Spanish church with her family a few times. Life seemed so simpler back then at least for me. I don't remember my Mom meeting Maria's parents, but I was always over there.

I remember walking home from her house. It was early in the afternoon. I went inside a corner store to get some candy before I made it home and when I came out of the store, there was this weird looking man. He had on a long black trench coat, a black hat, and black boots. He started to follow me, walking fast behind me, telling me to come here and that he had something to show me. I got scared and began to run. I ran into this ladies house. *Thank God for protecting me again.* Her front door was unlocked. She jumped up from her chair; she was watching, *'The Price Is Right.'* I remember the host saying, *"Come on down"*... The lady asked me *what was wrong.* I closed the door and told her that a man was following me. My chest was beating fast. She looked out of the window, and she said she saw a man passing by walking fast, looking back at the house. She confirmed that I was being followed. She offered to drive me home; I only lived a few blocks away. I didn't know the name of the street I lived on, but I knew how to tell her my left from my right. She never asked to speak to my Mother, to tell her "*your child just burst into my home saying she was being followed.*" She just told me '*to be careful out here walking by myself.*'

One day we were hanging with Maria's older sister and brother. They had us walking all over the place. We ended up by some railroad tracks where there was a swing and a slide set. There was a tunnel for a train to go through. We walked in the tunnel, not knowing what was in there or what could happen. Then I remember smelling this foul odor. As we were walking, I saw a dead body of a man with his face all eaten up. I guess it's from rodents. He still had his clothes on. He could have been homeless also. We just stood there looking at this dead body. It was getting dark, so I knew I needed to get home, and I had no idea where I was. Then all of a sudden, another man came running from the other end of the tunnel screaming at us. He told us "*that we did not belong here and that we better leave now before something happened to us.*"

The next thing I knew… I just took off running. I got split up from Maria and her siblings. As I was trying to find my way home, I noticed I had to cross the busy highway to get to the other side *to get home*. I am a little girl living this crazy and fast life. I basically did what I wanted to do. I remember running on the highway, cars honking their horns and everything!! It was four lanes across, and I was waiting until I could continue to cross the road to get to the other side of the highway. *Can you picture that*?! When I finally arrived home, it was dark. No one asked me anything about my day or my whereabouts. I didn't bother to say anything about playing at the railroad tracks, the dead body, or being followed. I didn't even mention being fondled by Mr. Timmons. I had no problem keeping secrets from my parents. I learned that early on.

Sexual Assault Facts

"It is estimated that at least two out of every ten girls and one out of every ten boys are sexually abused by the end of their 13th year.

To protect all children, we first need to learn the facts.

Did you know that most children who are sexually abused, are abused by a family member or close friend? Did you know that "stranger danger," by comparison, is quite rare"?

~Child Molestation Research & Prevention Institute

It's through sharing our wounds to childhood choices and chances that we unite to spark awareness in all efforts to help heal our nation of sexual assault
~Tamiko Lowry-Pugh

CHAPTER 5
Still Exposed

We moved again later that year to another apartment complex on the Westside of Colorado. The school year was about over. We moved so much I thought that was a normal thing to do. I remember giving some of my classmates the chicken pox. I had sores all over my body and inside my throat; I was out of school at least three weeks. I couldn't eat any salty spicy or hot foods, so *Jell-O, popsicles, and pudding it was.* No telling where and how I contracted the pox but the school nurse called my Mother for her to come and get there *real FAST*. I wasn't supposed to have company while my parents were at work, let alone, while I was infected with chicken pox. But did I listen, *of course not*. I was only nine years old. So my three friends, who were also *Mexican* and *I just knew I could speak some Spanish*! I would mock them and start saying things as if they could understand me. They would laugh at me, correct me and tell me "*no Me Me,*" say it like this… Robin, Brenda, and Steven came over a few times during my stay at home with the chicken pox. They eventually caught the chicken pox also and passed it around to their family members. *That was funny to me.*

When I was well enough, and I knew better not to go inside anybody's home at that time because I didn't want to go through that again. My Mother's bedroom door had a hole so big that my face could fit through it. I believe the hole was already there before we moved in. One day, I put my face through it, and I noticed they were having sex, doggy style at that. *You can already picture what I saw*. My Mom looked up and saw me watching them, so I ran to the bathroom and sat on the toilet seat with the lid down. My Mother came in, *"What are you doing?"* I said, *"Using the bathroom,"* acting like I was sleepy. *"With the toilet lid down?"* I can see her facial expression to this day. She yelled at me and told me to take my *"little ass to bed."* So after that day, they stuffed a pillow in the hole, I was already exposed to so much already.

My Mother told me that I had to start doing more for myself. I already knew how to cook eggs, and noodles. But now I knew how to make pancakes, bacon, spaghetti & meatballs. I could clean up, vacuum, wash clothes, and iron by the age of nine years old. What my Granny had shown me was a good start.

I remember the first time I burned my damn hand and my leg. Even to this day, I still see the burn mark on my leg; which is why I do not iron as much. We didn't have an ironing board, so it was done on a bath towel or a bed sheet that we put on the floor.

My Mom showed me at the age of nine years old, also, how to pick up my little brother, *Jr.* from an *In-home* daycare. I had to walk about ten blocks there and ten blocks back to get my brother. He was only one year's old at the time, in a stroller. The damn thing broke in the middle of the street… I had to cross a very busy street like *Peachtree Street or Candler Road*. I can laugh at it now, but I had to stop and fix the stroller in the middle of the street. The material came off from the metal part of the seat. I didn't know any better because I did all I could trying to fix it. All of that in the middle of the street, with the cars honking and people yelling at me, *"Where is your damn Mother?"* and *"You are a baby pushing a baby!"*

    I was made to mature early. I started my period at the age of nine years old too. I remember I was outside skating with some friends, and I fell, did the split around a pole, and hit my vagina. I was crying! My Mom came in the bathroom with me and looked between my legs and *'yes, I was bleeding.'* My Mom said to wait a few days to see if the bleeding would stop and it did but came back the following month. I remember the first day of school; I was starting the sixth grade, and my Mother had to tell the teacher I had my menstruation. I was too young to understand any of this stuff but all my Mother always told me about it was *"to keep clean"* and if I didn't, I *would smell like a dead fish*! Oh, and that *"I can have a baby now."* Why would she say that*?! I later found out what she meant by that, though.*

    I bled on myself one day in school, and some kids made fun of me. I thought I was special because I didn't know anybody else who had their period so young. So one day, this young girl, wanted to fight me because I had my period before her. Her name was *Martina* and she had an older brother. He told me that If I beat his sister up, that he was going to *kick my ass*. So I went down to her neighborhood all by myself. I didn't have any cousins or any friends to have my back. But one friend told me not to fight. His name was *David Bacon*. We would make fun of each other's last names '*Bacon and Bean.*' I always wondered if David is related to Kevin Bacon, *just a thought*. I had been through enough already so I was far from being scared. I was ready! Martina was talking and cursing at me in Spanish. I don't know what she was saying, but all I knew was she got in my face, and my hands started flying on that head. I was pulling her hair, and she was hollering for me to stop. It was just like how you see on the internet with *World Star Hip Hop*. With the girls fighting. If only we had that back then. *I beat her ass*! Her right eye was swollen, her lip was bleeding, and her hair was looking bad. Her brother tried to start with me, but some other kids said it was a fair fight. The word got around that I beat up Martina. Come to find out, that she was a force to be reckoned with, and I whipped her butt! I was only nine years old going on ten!

I befriended some other girls. Lauren was a tall white girl with blond hair and had blue eyes and Shelly, she was this mixed chic, her parents were white and black, she had short dark hair and was cross-eyed. We called ourselves starting a gang; we were called "*The Baby Dolls*" We all had blue jean jackets, and we wrote the name of the gang in a black marker. My initiation was to go to the corner store and while the other gang members distracted the person on the register. I had to steal a six pack of coke a cola. We all went to the store and the clerk already knew what was up. He yelled at us '*to get out of the store*', and while the other girls were messing with him, I took the cans of sodas right out of the 'fridgerator and ran out of the door and down an alley. Here comes the rest of the crew. We were laughing, but I was scared. Now nobody would ever mess with me.

Well, my parents found out. I'm not sure who told them, but school was all most out for the summer. And do you know what my punishment was, *I had to go to Granny's house for the summer*. I haven't seen her in two years, since the incident. From my understanding, her and *Cunningham* had broken up. *I wonder why*. She missed me, I guess; well she acted like she did. I didn't feel any type of way when I saw her. But when she saw me, she was smiling real hard showing her gold gap tooth, with her blonde hair and her big booty. My Granny was a pretty chocolate woman; *I have to say*. She started talking to me saying, *that she missed me* and how much *I'd grown*. She even said *'you have breast'* as she pinched them. Then she said *'I heard you got your period'* and saying the same thing that my Mother told me, "*You can have a baby now… so keep your legs closed*!" I didn't understand why she told me what *she heard* knowing that damn well my Mom told her. But she never once mentioned anything about me being molested in her house where I had to go back to and stay for three months. She made sure that I helped her "*clean up the house*," she would say, and I was busily thinking, *'it's not even any of my mess.'*

But I was happy. I got to visit my friend's *Dawn and Paula*. I was so glad to see them and their Grandmother, she just loved me, and the girls knew it. She knew my birthday was coming up and wanted me to celebrate it at their house. She had opened a hair salon in the upstairs part of the house where I was able to help with washing a few clients' heads. I learned how to roller set, and I had to clean up the stations. I also made some tips too. Dawn and Paula had an older sister. She was eighteen years old. Her name was *Stacy*, and she was dating this guy named Chester. He was nineteen years old. Stacy was going to have a baby by him.

Chester was so nice to me, calling me *'Lil Sis'* saying he would beat anybody ass if they ever tried to mess with me. He always wanted me to give him a hug and for me to give him a kiss on his cheek whenever we would see each other. We could be walking down the street or see each other at the corner store.

One day, I was at the hair salon, and Chester came in there with a box of hair supplies to be put away and saw that I was sweeping up some hair that was on the floor from earlier. When he entered the room, he was happy to see me, and I was happy to see him in a sisterly way. Well, he picked me up around my waist and started swinging me around saying, '*Hey Lil Sis*' and was kissing me all my over the face but not my lips. I thought it was funny. Then he puts me down when he heard someone coming up the stairs. So Dawn walked in and said she wanted me to stay for dinner. I called my Granny and asked her if I could '*stay down there to their house for dinner.*'

When I walked in the dining room, everyone started singing "*Happy Birthday*" to me. There was a cake on the table. I was so excited. *I wondered what my Mother was going to do for my birthday*!

I woke up early on that Saturday morning ready to go over to Dawn and Paula's house again because today was their sister's baby shower. But first, my Granny wanted me to go with her to the dog tracks. Yes, a child that goes to the dog tracks! I'm a just a little girl. She had me pick a few dogs names out while we were on our way. My Granny loved to gamble! Then she would spend all day at a few yard sales. We were always going to yard sales; we even set up a few in her front yard. Finally, we made it back; it was all dark outside. I was still allowed to go down the block because I was staying the night! As I was walking down the block, I could hear the music coming from inside of Dawn's house; she yelled out to me '*that I missed the baby shower, but they were still partying.*' It was a lot of people over there. When I walked in the house, you could smell the weed, and people had cups of alcohol in their hands. This was not my first party; *my Mom got down too now.*

Paula came up to me dancing and handed me a red cup. I began to dance too *and* took a sip of what was in the cup. It had alcohol in it because I had drunk some before with Cunningham. As I was walking through the house, people were everywhere, dancing, talking, eating and making out. Then Chester came up to me and picked me up like he always did. He said he had something to give me and told me to pull on this 'joint.' That was my first time smoking weed. I was only ten years old. I believe Dawn, Paula, and I were the only kids there; it was all adults, otherwise. I knew they had to be at least twenty years old or even older. Chester had me sit on his lap. Then he kissed me on my mouth this time and told me that *he loved me.* I guess I was buzzing. I had to be drunk and high. I didn't know how to feel or what to say. I was an easily gullible child. Later on when the party ended, and we were cleaning up, their Mother told me that I had to make a pallet on the floor in the den. While everyone was sleeping, Chester came into the den where I was sleeping. He laid down next to me and said that I am not his *Lil Sis* anymore, that I was his *secret little girlfriend* now. So he leaned over and kissed me again on my mouth this time, and I wasn't scared of him. He started rubbing on my vagina. I felt powerless, and I didn't bother to stop him.

I already had started my period and was in a '*b sized cup bra.*' I looked older for my age, but I was still a little girl. I liked the feeling, and I didn't see anything wrong with it. He then told me not to say anything because people would not understand our relationship.

Another time I stayed the night, and this time, I slept upstairs in the girl's room. While everybody was asleep, here comes Chester. He laid on the floor next to me again. He said to me that he loved me and he had to show me something. He kissed me on my mouth. Then he pulled out his penis and told me to hold it with my hands and to stroke it. I did it, and I wasn't scared at all this time. *I don't know why?* Maybe his approach was different from *Cunningham's* or maybe he wasn't so old or maybe my hormones were kicking in now; *from my understanding.*

Chester got on top of me and told me to '*be still.*' He said he was not going to hurt me. He began to put his penis inside of me. It hurt really bad. I liked this feeling because I didn't tell him to stop. I could have screamed, but I didn't, because Dawn and Paula were lying right in the same room as we were. When he finished, he told me that he loved me and for me not tell anyone. I went to the bathroom and set on the toilet, wiped myself and there was blood coming from my vagina. *It was like the time when Cunningham molested me.* I just sat there thinking about what just happened and hearing my Mom and my Grandmother's voice saying '*that I can have a baby now.*' I'm having sex at the age of ten years old. *I never told anyone.*

God made you my DAD.
LOVE made me your FRIEND.

CHAPTER 6
I'm Going Back to Cali

It was 1984, and I was *ready to go back* to Los Angeles that summer! I loved to see my Father's side of the family. I had a Madea. *My Grandmother*, before *Tyler Perry made his Madea*. She always took care of me when I came to visit. To this day, I believe that I was her *favorite grandchild*. She told us that we lived in a brown brick house back in the '70's. It had a large porch that wrapped around the house. If you know how some of the houses look in Los Angeles, then you have an idea. I was told that we lived across the street from *Tito Jackson's girlfriend, Michael Jackson's brother*. I do remember playing ball in the street with a bunch of boys and we chased each other around outside. But after all, it is Los Angeles, so you never knew who your neighbors were. That's my story, *and I'm sticking to that!* My Father tried his best to be a good Father and expose me to different things, *nothing like in Denver*. My Father loved me so much. I never saw my Dad drink or smoke anything until later on in my life. In Los Angeles, it was the beaches, the sand, blue water, the palm trees, always sunny and the Hollywood hills.

Now I'm with my cousins, *Tiff, Bob, Ran, and Ruben*. We were always together. Especially Tiff and I. My Auntie Benny (which is one of my Dad's older sisters), I stayed with them most of the time during the summer and two years of school, which I appreciate and loved her for that. We went to church a lot. *Wednesdays, Fridays, and Sundays*. Most of my family went to the same church. My uncle Bob was the Pastor. He was one of my Dad's older brother's. My Father never attended church, only when I was getting baptized. I was baptized more like *three times* throughout my years and speaking in tongues by the age of nine years old.

When we were at church on some Fridays nights, my Aunt would be up in the choir stands singing. She would see us acting up, so she would point at us. She was always threatening us; saying that she was going to '*spank our asses*' if we kept talking and playing in church. *But she never did.* I loved this lady. She helped my parents take care of me and spoiled the heck out of me as well. But nobody to this day is aware that I was ever molested. *Until they read this book*. We stayed in Cerritos California, in a three bedroom apartment complex. It was a nice part of town. My Aunt made sure we were comfortable. My cousin and I shared a room, and we had a '*girly room*' too with our *daybeds* and *stuffed animals* and with our favorite colors for the bedding. My cousin had a record player and, of course, we played *Michael Jackson and Prince* all the time.

One day, my cousin told me to listen to this record and she played the song "*Erotic City*" by *Prince*, his '*Purple Rain*' album backward and my Aunt heard it… she came running into our room saying "*turn that crap off 'cause it sounds like devil worship music.*" But we still snuck and listened to it anyway. My Father had received three concert tickets to *Michael Jackson's* "*Victory Tour.*" We had a blast! I remember crying because we got to see the '*Jackson Five*' and we had some real good seats at that! Even though we didn't get home until one or two a.m., we could not stop talking about the concert, and we deiced to write *Michael Jackson* a letter saying that *'we knew you many years ago, we love you and hope you remember us.'* But who were we? We still had to go to school. I didn't mind though because I got to brag about going to the concert!! I loved that the schools were very diverse too. I had friends of all races.

I had my first real kiss by a boy named *Lorenzo*. He was a Mexican and was handsome to me. It's like I blacked out. I remember getting ready to put my lips on his lips, and that's all remember. I know it had to be funny to my cousins; she timed us kissing and said it was for *fifty-eight* minutes *nonstop*. I was too nervous to pull away. I do not ever recall kissing that long to any man since then.

My Father stayed with my cousins' Godfather named *David*. My Father was his caretaker, and he took real good care of him too. He was disabled from the neck down. I believe he was in a car accident. He could feed himself, but the way he had to go to the bathroom was by using milk cartons to *pee* in. He had a blue van. It was comfortable for my cousin Tiff and me to ride in. My Dad and David and I always went to nice places; restaurants, movies, and shopping. I remember one time when we were leaving a restaurant, my cousin and I took some tip money that was left on a few tables. I know that was wrong. I was a little bad *sometimes*. My Dad was a light skinned man with a bald head. He had freckles, red hair, and his eyes were crossed-eyed. When he was a young boy in Texas, he was shooting a bow and arrow in the air and as it came back down and it hit him in his right eye. I believe he was about five years old at the time. That's where most of my looks come from; *him*. When my Father was 18yrs old, he worked as a cashier at a burger joint that was robbed. He was held at gunpoint and hit on the head with the butt of a gun, which later caused him to have a blood clot on his brain. He never went to see a doctor. I believe the brain injury made him a *little crazy*! I heard that my Dad had different odd jobs like working in an office building. I am not sure what he did. I saw him a few times in a suit going to work, he even did a little lawn care and worked on cars. He mainly had women customers. My Dad didn't care about impressing anyone on how he dressed. He wore only these karate pants and karate shoes. *He thought he was Bruce Lee*. My Father was a handsome man and the ladies loved some Ken. But his real passion was working on cars.

My Grandaddy Lester (not sure if he was my real grandad, this is what my Grandmother Dorothy Mae had told me ten years ago), but he owned an auto shop, so my Father worked there from time to time until my Grandaddy sold it. My cousin and I use to go with him to work and answer the phones and make coffee. Acting like this was our job, *pretending to be Secretaries*. My Father used to tell me crazy stories that he had special powers. He said that he once flew in the air, and stopped a train from running onto the Los Angeles traffic. He stated that he had a third eye, and so do I! And for me to look at him and he will show me, but I declined to look at him. From my understanding, that that is true; that people have a third eye. My girlfriend *Susan* said it is called '*Chakra*' which is linked to the pineal gland, located in the center of our brain between the left and right side. Which basically means your spiritual energy. He would eat his boogers, and he kept several pickle jars of his urine!! And to find out, also, there was a meaning behind this… I asked him '*why does he do that?*' He said, "What comes out had to go back in!" I loved my Dad, but he was a little crazy, *I must say*. It wasn't his fault. My Father used to get us up extra earlier in the summer mornings to teach us karate moves, and we had to jog three times around the block, and he even had me walk on his back! And he introduced me to *avocados* which are my favorite Mum! I ended up staying in California a little longer. My Mother asked my Dad and my Madea if I could. So my Aunt said, *'I could stay with her because my cousins and I are the same age.'* I had to attend school for a semester.

My parents divorced after two years of marriage. My Mother couldn't handle that my Father was a lazy Mama's boy. My Dad would do his best to help my Mom by sending her money to take of my needs (school supplies, clothes, hospital bills). He even drove to Denver twice to spend time with me.

My Father was shot six times and died in 1994 when I was eight months pregnant. He was planning to come and help me with his first grandchild. The last time I talked to him was on a Thursday, and he was going to call me that weekend. When I heard the phone ringing, it was on a Saturday; my husband answered it. I heard him talking, so I thought it was for him. But it was my Grandmother Madea calling to tell my husband that my Dad was found dead. My husband came into the bedroom and woke me up. I thought he was trying to have sex with me. He said, "*Wake up baby… give me a hug,*" I was like, "*Honey, no… my stomach is hurting because your son won't stop flipping around.*" He started to pull me close to him now; holding me "*That was your Grandmother Madea calling to tell you your Father was found shot dead in his car slumped over the steering wheel. He was shot six times!*" He was in an area in Los Angeles where drugs were sold and where hookers walked the streets. A nineteen-year-old drug dealer was trying to make my Dad take some free crack, (*I guess he was trying to get my Father back on drugs*). My Father was sitting in his car, got mad and pushed the boy a few times, and the boy fell to the ground. Then the young boy got back up, and pulled out a gun and started shooting at my Father, and one of the bullets hit him in his chest and killed him.

I remember when I went to Los Angeles to visit my Dad a few years before this, he looked awful. His teeth were black and chipped; he looked dirty! Like a crack head. I asked him what was wrong with him. He looked like he was on drugs. I was so hurt, I cried for hours. My husband had to call the paramedics because I was so far along in my pregnancy; he wanted to see if they could prescribe something to me that I could take to calm me down. One of the paramedics actually talked to me for a while… It seemed like they were there for hours, but I'm sure it was just a few minutes, but said *"that I am too far along to take anything… so I have to relax, or I could hurt the baby*, so eventually I relaxed and cried myself to sleep.

My family had a lovely funeral that I could not attend because again I was too far along, in the pregnancy, to fly on the airplane. My cousin *Tiff* made me this very beautiful book on my Dad's life and death with pictures of him, guest names, the pall bearers, and poems. I still look at it from *time to time*, smile and cry EVERY TIME whenever I *do* bring it out, to fondly remember my Father. Boy did he have his weird ways!

Can a Mother forget the baby at her breast and have no compassion on the child she has born? Though she may forget, I will not forget you!

Isaiah 49:15

CHAPTER 7
A Baby Having a Baby

I'm back from California baby; about to start a new school year. It was 1984. I was twelve years old at this time. My Mother picked me up from the airport. When we arrived in front of the home they were living in, my brothers were outside playing with a black and white cocker spaniel. I asked, "*Mom is that our dog?*" she said, "*Yes we have a dog, and his name is Bandit,*" but of course when I met Bandit, he became my dog. The house was a two joining duplex right across the street from a grocery store.

I was told that we were in the process of moving soon. But this house had an up and downstairs. We stayed downstairs in a two bedroom unit with a curtain dividing the rooms and one bathroom. I had to share a room with my two brothers for the first time. The kitchen was all white. I remember my Mom showing me how to make shrimp egg rolls, homemade cakes, fried chicken, eggs, potatoes, and onions, *yummy*! I still cook that meal to this day. I also remember mice coming in the kitchen and my dog trying to catch them, so my Stepdad put out a few mouse traps. I even I had to dump a few myself, *yuck*!

Yes! We moved! A real home! I finally get my own room. We moved not too far from that duplex into this yellow and green house. It had a large front porch with two staircases. The one staircase one was in the front as soon as you first walk in and the second one was at the back of the house that lead to the kitchen. This house had four bedrooms, a huge living and dining room, a nice sized kitchen and a big backyard. I had *my dog* Bandit, two fish tanks, a turtle, and hamster. My bedroom was so beautiful. I even had a white and pink canopy bed with beautiful butterflies on it with a matching blanket. I also had a pink stereo that I received one year for Christmas, a lot of stuffed animals, two Barbie dolls, and a cabbage patch doll that I named Karle and posters of Michael Jackson, Prince, The group Debarge, Ralph Macho, Rick Springfield, all over my bedroom walls.

I was getting ready to attend *"Cole"* Middle School. I had to walk of course. I was very excited about getting older and making some new friends and I did make a new friend too, named *Michelle*. (We are still friends to this day). She was a beautiful brown skinned girl with shoulder length hair. I met her in our 7th-grade gym class. She lived with just her Mom who was a short lady; shorter than me and my Mother even. But she didn't take any mess from nobody! They lived in the projects which were about fifteen blocks to walk. I spent most of my time over their house and boy did we have some fun! She wasn't as boy crazy at that time as I was.

Michelle and her little cousin stayed the night at my house one night, and we were about to give her a bath when the little girl locked herself in the bathroom with the water running in the tub. We could not open the door! So I had to go next door to get help. I heard rumors about this neighbor, but I needed help. I knocked on the door, and he answered it in his underwear. I told him what was going on and can he help me. This fool said to me, *"what am I going to do if he helps me?"* I told him not a *"damn thing."* He pulled out his penis anyway and told me that I had to give him *"head,"* or he was not going to help me. I was a little scared but was determined that I was not going to let anything happen this time. *I was so tired of being violated.* His wife's car pulled up. I was so happy! I ran up to her car, and she asked me *"what was I doing over here?"* while her husband was standing in the doorway still in his underwear not *saying anything.* I didn't say anything about what just happened... I just told her what was going on over at my house and that I came over here *"to get some help."*

I knew she didn't like my friend and me; I believe she was intimidated by us primarily because we were young teenagers and we had grown women bodies. She told her *no good husband* to get the key to unlock the bathroom door. I have never told anybody this story. I made it back inside my house... you could hear the little girl crying and Michelle sitting at the door talking to her; telling her we are going to get her out. I was able to open the door; the water was flowing over the tub. My parents never knew that I flooded the bathroom and thanked God the ceiling didn't cave in.

Then I met Bridgette walking to school on the first day of eighth grade. She ended up living with us for a little while. I thought to myself, *I finally have a sister now*. She had a few things going on at home as well. My parents were trying to be real strict on us. It's like the older I got, the more I was on punishment. I had all this freedom when I was younger, and now they want to lay out some rules! My goodness...*what*! They did not think that I was going to grow up! I had a crush on these two boys; they were first cousins. One of their names was Darnell, and the other one's name was Tony. He was very tall and slim with a long jerry curl, green eyes, and a big nose!

I like the way he talked. Michelle did not like Tony that much. She would say *"he is so ugly and his nose is so big."* But she liked Darnell who was dark skinned tall, and had a short haircut, muscles, juicy lips, a nice smile and was also bowlegged.

Our Mothers met a few times, and I was allowed to hang out with him only if his Mom was around. We would talk on the phone all the time and pass notes in the hallways at school and would make googly eyes at each other. I don't remember how the conversation came about, but one day Darnell and I decided that we were going to have sex.

We walked everywhere in Denver. Rain, sleet or snow! Even miles. It didn't even faze us. Darnell walked to my house to get me. He only lived about a mile away from me. When he arrived, I noticed that he had picked some flowers from somebody's yard. I don't remember us walking back to his house. I was floating on love. I was just happy to be next to him. He was just gorgeous to me! We knew each other several years ago. He lived in a gray and white house. His neighborhood set up looked so different from mine. His place inside didn't look as clean either. Inside smelled like feet and butt. They didn't have any furniture. It was just his little brother and his Mom. His Father had died from my understanding. I remember us going into his bedroom. We kissed a little bit and the next thing I knew, I pulled one leg from my pants, and he did the same thing. He climbed on top of me and put the head of his penis right on the opening of my vagina and with two or three pumps he said *"I came"* and *that was that*! We both were so hot. I guess he didn't know what to do and neither did I. He didn't even put his penis inside me. Then I said, *"what if am pregnant?"* I don't know why I said that. So we pulled our pants up, left his house and went to McDonald's to get something to eat, and he walked me back home. He apologized for what had happened and said, "*You aren't pregnant because I didn't put it inside of you.*" It is crazy on how I look back on my life and see how grown I was acting and how much freedom I had.

We went to school the following weeks; Darnell and I still flirted with each other in the hallways at school, but we didn't have any classes together. After what happened between us, nothing else transpired *yet*. So six weeks passed and *no period*! Plus, I started throwing up, and I started throwing away my pads. My Mother never questioned me about my period. So I told my Art Teacher, *Ms. Bennett*, that my period was late and that I might be pregnant!

A few days later, Ms. Bennett took me to the Eastside health clinic. She could have lost her job for taking me off the school premises. We had left a little bit before school was out. So here I am, *at the clinic*, and I have to tell the nurse what happened. But as I sat in the waiting room, I saw a lot of young girls with huge stomachs and some were holding little babies. I was praying, *please Lord don't let me be pregnant! How am I going to tell my Mom? I don't know anything about babies*! So the Nurse called my name, and we both followed her into an examining room. The Nurse asked me some questions, and I answered them. She was not shocked about me being there because the waiting room was filled with young Mothers and *Mothers-to-be*. A few of my friends already had babies. She examined me and asked me to urinate in a cup; so I did. Then the Nurse left the room for a few minutes. My teacher didn't say much. All she kept saying was "*you are a little girl, oh my god, let it be negative.*" The Nurse finally came back in with a "*YES... you're pregnant!*" Ms. Bennett started crying and my dumb ass was laughing. People said, I was in shock; that's why I was acting that way. So the Nurse gave me my next doctor's appointment and told me "*congratulations!*" Being sarcastic.

Ms. Bennett and I walked back to her car, and she started crying again. She said, "*You have to tell your Mom and then decide what you are going to do. Keep the baby or get an abortion.*" And I will have to tell Darnell so that he can tell his Mom. Ms. Bennett took me home, and she came in *to say hello* to my family and to confirm that I was able to stay next weekend with her at her apartment for a school project. My Mom liked her. This wouldn't be my first time staying at her place. It was an art show, and we went to a dog show that weekend. I guess she knew I need a different outlet. She was a cool lady and was concerned that I hadn't said anything to my parents yet about my being pregnant. She told me, "*Little lady if you don't told them real soon... I will have to come to your house and do it myself.*" Sunday night I was lying on Ms. Bennett's floor in a sleeping bag with my mind going a hundred miles an hour. I could not fall asleep, *at all*, just wondering if I kept this baby could I make in life. I was only thirteen years old going through this… *WOW!*

My stomach was hurting so bad by the time Monday morning came, and I hadn't told my parents yet. You know how you wrote letters in class to your classmates, fold them and draw designs like numbers and shapes on it. So my stupid ass again wrote a note to Darnell, passed it to him in the hallway when we changed classes telling him point blank that I was pregnant! A classmate took the note and passed it around, but nobody knew it came from me.

I had heard people talking about it… *that Darnell got someone knocked up*, and they were trying real hard to find out who the person was. I told my friend Monica that I was pregnant and she asked me, *what I am going to do*. I told her that, *I was going to keep it and that Darnell and I were getting married.* She just looked at me like I was crazy. That was how I met Monica, *for the first time*, in a math class. The kids always gave this one particular teacher the blues. I had on a dress and this boy named Quincy crawled under my desk trying to look up my dress. I saw him down on the floor. I had this black afro comb in my desk, so I took it out, and grabbed the back of his shirt, and started beating him in his head with it a few times. I told him, "*if you don't get your ass up off the floor! Don't try me today!*" That's when Monica came in. It was her first day at the school. She has been my friend ever since.

It was a crazy week at school, but the next day Darnell and I met up at the park before school to discuss what we were going to do with the baby. When I saw Darnell he had shaven all of his hair off, he looked so scared and stressed. We both agreed to tell our parents the following Monday after school. I know that sounded crazy, but we had a lot of activities that week.

I was helping Michelle and Bridgette with their 'Janet Jackson Control' talent show, bake sale, and a car wash. *So* the time was here to tell my Mother about the baby. It was after school, and I was always told not to bother my Mother while she is sleeping. Something I should have learned earlier, but the good child I am, I had to wake my Mother up.

I knocked on her bedroom door and let myself in. "*Mom,*" I said, "*wake up... wake up... I have something to tell you,*" she lifted her head up, "*What girl... this better be important.*" I just yelled it out, "*I am pregnant! I am having a baby.*" My Mother laid there for a few seconds, then she sat up, "*Are you playing with me?!*" because she knew I joked a lot. I said, "*Yes, Mom... I mean, 'no' I am not playing, but yes... I am pregnant! I am having a baby!*" but I was laughing, still in shock I guess. She started to cry real hard, and asked, "*who in the hell had I slept with!*" She already knew Darnell... so I told her what happened. She said go and get your Stepdad. He was outside working in the yard. So I ran downstairs, went outside and yelled, "*Tommy! Mom wants to talk to you!!*" I am still laughing and went back upstairs before he came into the house. When he made it upstairs, he said, "*Yea, babe what's up?*" My Mother looked at me, and she told me. "You tell him what you said to me!" So, I told him, "*I am having a baby!*" I was serious about this-this time and yelled out, "*I am going to keep the baby!!*"

I ran to my room crying and threw myself on my bed. I guess it finally hit me. For a few days, I had in my mind that I was going to be a "*Mommy.*" Darnell's Mom called my Mother, and they were coming over so we could discuss what we were going to do. When Darnell and his Mother arrived, he and I were sitting side by side each other, holding hands. *Wow,* I was thirteen, and he was fourteen. We both said we wanted to get married after high school. He was going to put off college for a year, and I was going to do the same. And we thought our parents were going to raise our child. That was our plan. Darnell's Mother said she would be there no matter what I decided to do.

So time went on, and I started having morning sickness. I didn't like that shit! Not one bit! My family decided to go out for dinner at Golden Corral and while we were standing in the line, all of a sudden I started feeling sick, my body was shaking, and I was sweating. I didn't know I was supposed to be eating throughout the day. All I ate *always* was *some breakfast*. My Mother followed me outside, and I vomited between two cars. *I threw up… threw up… the baby was hungry.* All I heard my Mom saying to me was "*this is what you want? You're going to be sick and the baby is going to get sick at times. You're going to be stuck raising this baby.*" She said I wouldn't be able to hang out with my friends, at all, because she was not going to be babysitting all the time. "*You are just a baby yourself!*" And she went *on and on* saying she loved me and she was also crying. I then started just crying and crying too and saying "*I don't want to be a Mother anymore I changed my mind, this is not fun at all!*"

So the plans changed. My parents talked me into getting an abortion! So my Mother called Darnell's Mom to let her know that I had decided to have an abortion and how much it would cost and what her half would be. This woman said she didn't '*believe in killing a baby*,' so she will not take part in that and '*we are on our own*'! My Mom cussed her out; called her a few choice words since this was the same woman who said '*she would be there for me no matter what we decided.*' So we had to call my Father and lie to him telling him I was having surgery on my hand. Nobody on my Dad's side of the family knew I was pregnant. I needed four hundred dollars; that's how much the procedure would cost. My Mother, Michelle and I went to the abortion clinic very early the next morning. It was in the summertime, June of 1985. I had to fill out some forms because my Mom wouldn't do it for me. She said this is your procedure. I was laying on her arm being a little girl saying, "*Mommy, please do this for me*." Soon we were escorted to the back room and waited again for a Nurse to come in. There was a magazine on the table with the story about a boy who was set on fire by his Father. I remember talking to my Mom about it. My Mom said "*the Father didn't want a divorce, so he was going make the boy's Mom suffer*," but the young boy survived.

The Nurse came in the room and explained what was going to happen and that this was a two part procedure. My Mom was able to stay for the first part. They inserted this stuff called seaweed into my uterus; the Nurse said 'it's going to make me cramp,' and 'dry the egg up.' So I had to leave it in there for a few hours and come back to finish the second part of the procedure. My Mom took us out to lunch at the Red Lobster. We didn't talk much; I was too scared to say anything. My girlfriend, Michelle, was still by my side. Later that day we went back, and they were ready for me. I was so scared. Nobody could go in the back with me this time. *Here we go*. I had to lie on this hospital bed and put my legs in the stirrups. The Nurse had everything set up. It was a machine that had a hose attached to it. So the nurse told me to relax and take deep breaths while she inserted the hose inside my vagina and she turned it on!

It sounded like a vacuum cleaner. That shit hurt like crazy. All I wanted to do was jump off this damn bed! I felt it pulling on the inside. It was sucking the egg out; getting any sign of the fetus out… that's what the Nurse said. All I was thinking about as I lie, there was '*why did I do this to myself?*' I am never going to have sex again! Plus the sad part of it all was that he just placed his penis on the opening of my vagina. I was trying to hold back my tears as I still felt it pulling on inside me.

The Nurse said I was *"finished!"* Yes! It's was over. I was able to *cry a little bit finally.* She explained that I would bleed for a week like '*I'm on my period.*' I cleaned myself up, got dressed, came out of the patient's room and walked back in the front area where my Mom and Michelle had been waiting for me. Michelle got up and gave me a hug, "it's *going to be alright.*" My Mom didn't give me a hug but she did say, "*I bet you won't go through this again*" and to this day, I sure the hell did not! But I couldn't even be mad at my Mom, because, at the end of the day, she always had my back! So that was done! No one talked about what happened to me. Now back to being fast again.

Did you know?

Experiencing sexual assault can change a person's perception of themselves. Which can cause a breakdown in self-esteem and can lead to emotional bondage.

It also can affect the way an individual perceives relationships; causing them to become fearful or withdrawn.

~Meshia M. Bean

"Before I formed you in the womb I knew you, before you were born I set you apart; I appointed you as a prophet to the nations."
– Jeremiah 1:5

CHAPTER 8
Moving to Hotlanta

It was a new school year. My first semester of ninth grade. I was attending East High school with Bridgette. She had a boyfriend that picked her up sometimes, or she would stay the night over at his house. The school mascot was an Angel. East's colors were *"red and white,"* but the school was too far for me to walk to every day, so my Mother had to change my school and I went to Manuel High; which was a lot closer to my house. Their mascot was a *"thunderbolt"* and their colors were *"red, blue and white."* I tried to wear the school colors every day to school.

One evening walking home, I ran into *Tony*! I liked him a lot; he was my first childhood love. I was in the ninth grade, and he was in the tenth. He would steal his Mother's car to come pick me up. We would go to the movies and out to eat. One day, when he was sneaking over to my house, he hit the curb and busted a tire. He had to call his Mother at work and tell her what had happened. She already knew why he took the car, of course; *he was coming to see me*. We knew his family also. He lived with his Mother and a younger brother; his Father was in jail for murder. He lived in a nice neighborhood; in a teal blue house. We had to grow up *oh so fast*. Tony and I started having sex at every chance we had alone. Our parents knew already, but they could not stop us from seeing each other. One time I was over his house, and we were in his Mom's bed having sex and didn't use any protection. After we had finished, I thought about how I could have gotten pregnant *again,* but that still didn't stop me.

We would go over to Michelle's house to hang out, and her Mom would say to us when she saw us kissing, that we were "*sucking face,*" mainly me, since I was doing all the kissing. She was so cool. I loved this lady so much. Michelle and I would meet up, and we would smoke weed on our way to school together almost every day. There was this club that we would also attend. It was in the projects very close to where Michelle lived. It was called "*Club Breezin.*" It was for ages fourteen to eighteen years old. We were so dang on grown. At least we thought we were. The crew would meet up at somebody's house or in someone's alley, and we would get bent, really "*wasted.*"

Michelle's Mom had this boyfriend that would get drunk and argue with her all the time. They would leave on weekends and would even leave us some weed, plus we already had some liquor hid in her closet. My parents used to sell and smoke weed as well. One day my Mother and I were just sitting around talking and out of nowhere I told my Mom that I knew how to smoke marijuana. I was fourteen years old. She didn't believe me so I showed her that I knew how to roll with white papers (5.0) and I smoked it with her. She tried to get mad and said she was going to send me back to California, but I told her I learned it from them.

I used to sell my parent's weed at school. I would have dollar joints and two dollar joints; already rolled up, and hide them in a wide medicine container. One day, it was lunchtime, and the school was allowed to leave the premises for an hour for lunch. So

Michelle, Monica, and I were in the alley behind this burger place called *"Brown Sugar's"* it was across the street from our high school. We had a park across the street also. It was something we did all the time during our lunch break, then come back to class high; *I failed my science class by the way.* I had my large black purse with the weed in it, and I was about to pull out the container, and here come my parents riding up the alley! I dropped my purse like a big dummy and ran inside of the burger place. I should have just stood there like nothing was going on, but I knew I was doing wrong.

My Stepdad came in, walked up and just looked at me, and angrily pointed his finger at me, putting it right on the tip of my nose and said to me in front everybody, *"the cops are down the street, and I should get them,"* to teach us a lesson! But instead, he added, "I will see you at home!" I could have shitted on myself. But nothing happened when I arrived home, they both said *"We know you are going to experience things but do it inside not outside and be smart about how and where I do things,"* but they were selling anyway so why not follow in their footsteps. I had let my son drink a beer with me when he was sixteen years old. I didn't see anything wrong with it because he was with me. I tell my son the same thing as well, be smart how you handle your business because people in this world are crazy! Thank God, I didn't have worry about my child. He doesn't care about all that partying and drinking.

I remember my parents splitting up, and my Stepdad had moved out of the house and my Mom and brothers stayed the weekend over at his new place. Bridgette and I decided to have our boyfriends Tony and Dennis come over on a Sunday evening. We had the music playing, some candles burning, and the guys brought the alcohol and chicken wings. We sat around looking at each other like we didn't know what to do. Bridgette had us play '*spin the bottle*.' Somehow, someone made a move and the next thing I knew, Tony just dove on top of me and was kissing me so fast. I was shocked; it wasn't like this was our first time together. I started laughing hysterical, telling him that it was tickling me. As I fell on the floor, I looked over at Bridgette and Dennis. Bridgette was twerking on Dennis's lap as Prince's '*Let's go crazy*' song was playing. I went to the kitchen to get some cups for the drinks and the phone rang. Thank God, we had the caller "ID," the one you had to plug the adapter into the phone, where the name and number will pop up. It was my Stepfather's name that came up, so I ran into the front room to tell the boys to be quiet. *How crazy were we to have boys over at the house, like we were grown*? I answered the phone; it was my Mother calling us, telling us to get ready for school tomorrow, and not to stay up late. She heard the music in the background and asked, "*What are you guys doing?*" I said, "*Nothing just listening to some music and making some dinner.*" Then she asked to speak to Bridgette.

And before she hung up, she said, "*And you better not have any company over there!*" I said, "*Yes Mama, I know better.*" Myself today, I would have driven my butt over to check up on the kids knowing my past! *You knew what I mean.*

So back to the boys! I told them that the coast was clear. I remember we were drinking some alcohol called "*night train.*" It was known as a wino's drink. We were all playing around and kissing. I was getting drunk; Tony was grabbing on me, and I was pushing him away, running around the house. The four of us ended up putting on the first Ghostbuster movie on a VHS cassette tape. Tony and I went upstairs. We slept in my parent's bed. I am sure we had sex. We were like rabbits anyway. I don't know what time the boys left or if I let him out but the next thing I knew, my Stepdad came home, and he came into their bedroom and saw that I was sleeping in their bed. He yelled my name, "*Meshia! What the hell are you doing in here and why aren't you at school?*" He just knew Bridgette was at school. He went to her room and was surprised to see her sleeping as well. He was like, "*If ya'll don't get your asses up and get dressed for school…*" It was already nine-thirty, so we were late. He told us that he was not even going to write an excuse for us *for being late*. But that was cool because Bridgette always wrote our school notes if we needed one.

Then one day, I was looking for something in my parent's room. I looked under the bed, and I saw a round can directly in the center of the bed. I got the broom and scooped it out from underneath it. The can had a photo of cookies on the outside, but when I opened it, to my surprise it was a can filled with naked Polaroid pictures of my Mom and Stepdad having sex! I remember seeing one picture of my Mother with her butt up in the air and it a happy face made out of it from a can of whip cream.

When my girlfriend's Michelle, Bridgette and I skipped school, one day, I was so silly, I showed them the photos that I had found of my Mother and Stepdad posing naked, and showed them the sex tape that they had made of themselves as well, along with other porn tapes.

My Stepdad injured his hand at work and while we were waiting on the settlement, my parents decided that we are moving to Atlanta, Georgia! I could have died. I had to leave all of my friends and my boyfriend and the worst part of it all; we ended up watching the movie about the Atlanta child murders! I remember running out of the house screaming to the top of my lungs saying that they are going to get me too. I was teased by some my classmates when they heard that I was moving to Atlanta, Georgia, saying, "*If I go… that I might be next.*" I didn't want to leave my boyfriend, and when I saw Darnell in the hallway at school, he had stopped me. We had seen each other, but we hadn't spoken since the abortion in the eighth grade. He asked me was it true that I was moving away? I said, "*Yes,*" then this fool told me, *I wish you would have kept the baby so you wouldn't have had to leave, and we would be together.* The next thing I knew, I slapped him across his face so hard that my hand was stinging so I can imagine how his face felt. I told him you can go to hell and I walked away. I saw him again about twenty years later, and he apologized for his *and* his Mother's actions back then. It took me many years to stop thinking about what I went through and how my life would have been as a VERY young Mother. I only can imagine what other young ladies went through and are still going through.

I could have stayed with my Granny, but I didn't want to. I pretty much stayed away from her house *anyway*. One morning on my way to meet up with Michelle like we always did, I noticed she looked sad. I asked her what was wrong and she started to cry and said they were moving back to Baltimore. All I could do is give her a hug like she gave me. I was like, "*we are both moving.*" We went on with our day, and after school, we were playing in the sprinklers at the park and later went to my house to change clothes. I went to open my bedroom door and my play Uncle was on his knees, kneeling down at my door, we would throw our clothes in the middle of the hallway and push them down the back stairs so they could be washed, but he moved from the door so fast. I closed the door, looked at Michelle and asked her if he was peeking through the keyhole. She said, *"Yes."*

My bedroom door had a skeleton key hole, so it was big enough for him to see us real good. I didn't say anything to my Mom at that time. I told my school counselor, and she advised me to tell my Mother. So I did. She asked my Uncle about it, and he said he was getting the clothes together to be washed, and said I was saying that because I didn't want to move to Atlanta! He still says that to this day. My Mom believed him. One day my Mom and I were in the car coming from the store. I told her, *"I am not going to go through this again,"* and I told her, *"If he touched me, she was going to have a dead brother lying next to her!"* She didn't say anything to me.

One snowy evening, my stepdad decided he wanted to take the family along with my play Uncle who was acting anxious, up to the mountains in the snow. I thought he was going to kill us! Michelle and I. But we ended up at this seafood restaurant. As we were getting ready to start to pack up, my parents had to go to Georgia to find a place for us to live. I had to keep one of my brothers, but I had my Aunt Vicki keep him for a couple of days. Monica came banging on my door, one night, so I opened the door, and she hurried up, rushed in and said, *"Close the door... I just ditched a cab."* We did that a lot back then.

The cab driver came knocking on my door asking, *"Did a young black girl come in here?"* I said, *"No,"* and that, *"you have the wrong address!"* The things *we* did. My friends and I partied *since*

I was moving to another State that kidnaps black children anyway.

Sexual Abuse Warning signs in children and adolescents

Children often show us rather than tell us that something is wrong.

What to watch out for in children:
- Acting out in an inappropriate sexual way with toys or objects
- Nightmares, sleeping problems
- Becoming withdrawn or very clingy
- Becoming unusually secretive
- Sudden unexplained personality changes, mood swings and seeming insecure
- Regressing to younger behaviors, e.g. bedwetting
- Unaccountable fear of particular places or people
- Outburst of anger
- Changes in eating habits
- New adult words for body parts and no obvious source
- Talk of a new, older friend and unexplained money or gifts
- Self-harm (cutting, burning or other harmful activities)
- Physical signs, such as, unexplained soreness or bruises around genitals or mouth, sexually transmitted diseases, pregnancy
- Running away
- Not wanting to be alone with a particular child or young person

~Parents Protect

Some stories don't have a clear beginning, middle and end. Life is about not knowing, having to change, taking the moment and making the best of it, without knowing what's going to happen next.
-Gilda Radner

CHAPTER 9
All These Black People

Man, it took us three days to drive to Atlanta, Georgia. It was 1988. We were on the highway and the song *"Doin' the butt"* came on the radio. My parents were like, *"Welcome to your new home."* All I saw was black people! More than I have ever seen in one place. It was going to be my sweet sixteen birthday, and I had to spend it alone, aside from my parents and my little brothers. They bought me a cake and sang *"Happy Birthday* to me."

My Stepdad announced that my Uncle and his friend would be down here in a few weeks, and he will be staying with us from time to time. But didn't I tell them this damn man was peeking at me through my bedroom keyhole! *"What the hell."* We had to stay with my Stepdad's Mother for a few months. Of course. I wasn't happy to be away from what I was used to; moving from house to house in the same town is one thing, but moving to a whole new State, was an entirely different thing altogether. I told my Mom that '*I wanted to kill myself... that I didn't want to be here*.' I just had a freaking temper tantrum and told her that I missed my boyfriend and all my girlfriends. My Mother said that she '*would help me*,' and asked me '*how I wanted to die*.' I was shocked by her reaction so, you know, I change my mind *real fast*.

I was starting my tenth grade at a new high school. *Talk about being scared.* My stomach was in my throat; I was tired of always feeling like that; always afraid of starting something new. *No more*! There were so many black people all around. I was afraid of my own people;, especially at my high school. I meet two friend's though, one named *Regina* and the other *Nikole*, and the first thing I asked them was '*did they smoke weed*?' because I had a joint inside my hand held compact mirror. Nikole already had a purse full of different kinds of bottles filled with pills. She was selling already and later that week Nikole had some weed she brought to school for us to smoke. So after school, we went to a friend's house; *being grown* as usual. We were getting high, and the next thing I knew my heart started beating so fast, I was talking to myself saying "*Oh my God, I am about to die*." I told my friends that I could feel my blood running through my veins and it felt like it was boiling too! Nikole said that "*I was tripping out*," and they were laughing at me. She was like "*I promise you will not be smoking with me ever again*." It took hours for me to come down off my high. I made it home late, and I lied to my parents that I had to stay after school for a project that was due. Every time I said I would not get high again, *I did it anyway*!

One day I rolled up a joint with the weed we brought back from Denver, and my smart ass was smoking it on the front porch in front the door. My parents came home, and my Mother must have smelled it in the house because she came back outside and said to me, "*if you're going to smoke, at least don't do it front of the door*." I didn't know what to say, I just laughed to myself, the wind was blowing it back in the house.

We moved into our own house; which to this day my family still lives in. I was washing my hair at the sink, and I had on some shorts.

I felt a finger brush across the back of my leg, I jumped up and looked back, it was my play uncle! *Damn*!

Time went on... I started working at McDonald's, along with the singing group "*Silk*," before they were famous. I was downstairs in the storage room changing clothes, and I noticed some tennis shoes sticking out from the curtain. It startled me a little bit. I walked over to the curtain and yanked it open and hit *him* in his damn head. I'm not saying his name, but he thought it was funny, and after that, I could not be around him.

One day my Mom picked me up from work, and we were talking about boys. She asked me how I was handling what happened to me when I was a little girl? I asked her what was she talking about? She said his name, '*Cunningham*' and everything came rushing back to me. I had forgotten all about that. I had blocked it out. Now I was thinking about it every day. That job had closed down, and my Mom told me I had to find another job and don't come back home until I found one! I walked down to the mall, but nobody would hire me. My Mother told me that she found a job for me at a chicken place. So I went and made some friends at my new job, and I would stay a few a days over my girlfriend's *Geni's* house. When I came back home, I saw my Uncle with the dirty clothes basket... he was sniffing my underwear! He didn't see me, but I sure in the hell saw him... *with his nasty ass*! From that point, I would hide my panties in a brown paper bag, and I washed them myself.

I noticed when I closed my bedroom door, (I had two doors that led to my room, one that led to the front room, the other one led to the kitchen). I saw two holes that someone had drilled in my door.

Lights were piercing from the kitchen, so I opened the door and went into the kitchen and closed it. I got a step stool and climbed on it, and looked through the holes. I could see straight in my bed! This *'Motherfucker'* I said to myself. So I politely got some tissue and twisted it in the holes! I didn't say anything to my parents at that time. I could tell someone was going through my things, looking for my dirty underwear, so I left a note saying something like this... *"Whoever is going through my dresser, and snooping around my things, and smelling my panties, is a nasty son of a bitch! And I hope you die very slowly*!!"

I came home one day, and the note was gone. So somebody had to take it from my dresser. It was that damn pervert! If my Mother had found the note she would have said something to me, *I hope*. I was tired of feeling and being violated so I told my parents and they talked to that damn fucker. He said that '*he would not hurt me, that he loved me, and what can a little girl do for him.*' He ended up leaving, and I never saw him again!!

I meet my husband at the Marta Rail Station. I was walking when I saw this gorgeous muscled brown skinned man standing there holding two huge plants, and I said to myself, "*He is going to be my husband.*" We were dating *so so much* in love with each other. I was eighteen, and he was twenty-eight. Yes, I love my old men! He was working in the restaurant field as a chef, as a restaurant manager. He introduced me to different types of foods and taught me how to cook.

He lived in Techwood area by Atlanta Technical College, in a rooming house that was mice and roach infested but I stood by my man til the end. We had made love many times before, but this particular time, I had a flashback about my Step-Grandad on top of me holding me down, I freaked out, and I started fighting him, and pushing him telling him to get off of me! I know I must have scared the hell out of him. He suggested that I needed to go to counseling before this continues to ruin my life. But I didn't do that until years later. I say to all of this, *to say*, "It's ok to get some counseling." It doesn't mean that you are crazy, not by far, because that is what I thought, and I am glad I did. It took me thirty plus years to figure that out.

My ex-husband is a very smart man, and I had learned a lot from him. At the beginning of our relationship, we were baptized together, and read the Bible every day. Although he grew up as a Muslim, he changed his religion for his family. They say a family that' *prays together stays together*,' and we took that to heart but we started having problems in our relationship several years later. I was getting a little bored with it. I was still young, *I suppose,* and my nose was wide open. I was getting attention from other guys that I was wasn't getting at home but my husband wasn't hitting on me like what happened to my Mother.

All I wanted was some hugs and to be told I was beautiful sometimes, *just some appreciation.* I guess he felt if the bills were paid, that's all he had to do. But I tried to tell him, '*I am not a bill, I am your wife, and I have needs.*' We tried marriage counseling once or twice, but it didn't work. So I suggested that we should have a threesome, and he was ok with the idea at first, but soon after, he thought about it for a few weeks, and he was like, "*hell no!*"

We did create a beautifully made, smart and handsome son. One of the happiest moments in my life. My son wanted to be the first *Black President*, so my Mother started calling him "*Mr. President.*"

Mothers hold their children's hands for a short time, but they hold their hearts forever.

~Meshia M. Bean

CHAPTER 10
My Queen

She worked at a local Hospital as a Surgical Tech. My Mother was a devoted Christian. She loved the Lord so much; she called him her Daddy. She and another lady did a *deliverance* on me before. That was a sight to see. As they were praying over me to get over my fears of driving and to stop smoking and partying. They put a bucket in front of me so that I could throw up some evil spirit. *What demons was I supposed to throw up?* I was crying, and I was mad as hell, and thought to myself, I didn't have an evil bone in my body. That was one of the scariest moments in my life. But sure enough, I was driving a few weeks later… so something must have worked.

My Mother suffered from severe back pain from when she fell and fractured her shoulder in 2002, and then she found out that she had broken her neck. On July 11th, 2008, I woke up from my nap to get ready for work, and the first thing I always do is check my messages. To my surprise, my Uncle left a message saying that "*he loved my Mother and me.*" He was crying while he was talking, and said, "*I know she is in a coma*," but he was "*praying for her.*" I jumped out of my bed in disbelief not understanding what he was talking about! So the first thing I did was call my Stepdad while pacing back, and forth. He answered the phone, and I said, "*What is Uncle talking about that Mom is in a coma!*" He said, *Yes, it is true,*" and for me not to come down to the hospital until after work because "*there is nothing I can do at this time.*" He explained that due to an outpatient procedure there were complications and he was not sure what exactly happened. I was on the floor crying so hard that I couldn't see anything *at all*. But I had to get myself together for work; I did it, and it was hard as hell to concentrate. I cried all the way to work and during my shift. I tried to work and answer several phone lines, but I could not stay focused at all.

So that morning, when I got off of work I rushed to the hospital where my Mom was at. The car I was driving was a stick shift that my girlfriend Nikole's Mother let me borrow it for a while, and I really didn't know how to drive it, and it kept cutting off. *Remind you; I was driving with one eye*! So my dear friend Monica of thirty years from Denver, Colorado came to my rescue. She met me at this apartment complex. She drove the car I was driving, and I drove hers. When I arrived at the hospital, the lobby was filled with a lot of my Mom's friends. Some had brought food for us. I was very anxious as I walked into her hospital room where she was laying in the bed with all of these tubes and wires attached to her. She had to have a tracheotomy, (an incision in the windpipe made to relieve obstruction to breathing) and she was so swollen. I just broke down. It felt like I was being eaten up from the inside out! I could not stop the pain. I knew my blood pressure was sky high. You know, when you're in so much pain your eyes hurt also.

She was in a coma at least three weeks and was later moved to another hospital for six weeks. That was a horrible experience for her; she couldn't talk or move not even a finger, and we had to learn how to clean her up, even when she had a bowel movement. I remember the first time the nurse had to wipe her butt. She cried so hard because she was a very proud woman. She had dignity! But soon, she stopped crying because she knew she couldn't do it herself. One morning, I went to visit her at the hospital. Her room door closed. My Mother was laying in her feces that was left on her butt that looked like it has been there for a while. She was hollering because her ass was burning. I was so freaking LIVID! So I went the nurse's station yelling at anybody in my path, *"Why in the hell is my Mother's door closed?"* You know what the damn heifer said, *"Because she would be crying all the time."* I said, *"Of course she would be hollering because she has shit all on her ass!"* And I am sure it had to be burning her! *"If that was your Mother would you have been concerned about her?"* One of the nurses was about to give her a bed bath and just snatched the pillow from under her head and let it crash against the hard bed. The nurses would ask us to leave the room when it was time to bathe her... I would tell them *"No Mam,"* I said to them, *"This is my Mother, and you do not know her, so I am staying right her!"* So every morning, when I got off of work at eight a.m., I walked a mile to the hospital to visit my Mother. They didn't know who was going to show up. But they made sure she was bathed and cleaned because they didn't want the family to show out on them.

The family would take turns staying with my Mom. She was our rock, and she kept everybody together for the most part. Weeks later, she was moved to a Rehabilitation Hospital. (I loved this place, and I am also a patient there. Seen there also by a Neurologist for my Multiple Sclerosis). This place showed us how to care for my Mother and took very good care of her. One morning, I walked into the room and she was sitting up in her hospital bed smiling when she saw me and something didn't look right, I was smiling back at her and said, *"Mom,"* as I'm looking at her, *"where is your trachea?"*

All I see is a hole in her throat, and she is laughing so hard she had some drool running down the right side of her face, as I looked around, I saw this red cap on the floor that was supposed to be on my Mother's throat. As I pushed the call button for the nurse, I said to her, "*you coughed that thing out of your throat.*" We both were laughing so hard as I went to her, gave her a big kiss and a big hug and called her *my Queen.*

I told her she was my best *friend and my queen.* So the doctors checked her out, and they said she didn't need it anymore. Of course each passing day we thought she would be getting better. My job was not too far the hospital, so I would leave from there and go to work almost every night, and I would go back most mornings to see her, but I wasn't worried about her; she was in good care. My Mom stayed there for three months.

Eventually, we brought my Mother home from the hospital; they showed us how to take care of her. My Mother could not talk or walk or even move a muscle, but she could make a hell of a lot of noise by hollering! She had her same personality (laughing), but that woman would fuss until you get her together; she would have us crying because we could not figure out what was wrong with her. I would be sitting in a recliner right next to her bed watching *Steve Harvey* hosting *Family Feud*. While everyone is happy that she is finally home, we were still trying to build a routine for her and also working on a good way to communicate with her in her current state. Everything was fine, but out of nowhere, my Mother started yelling at the top of lungs. She was screaming so loud that it pierced my eardrums. I jumped up and tried to calm her down. Bad idea! She started yelling even louder with tears rolling down her face now.

Everyone by now came and rushed into the room standing over her. Seemingly agitating her even the more. Man, I never knew a person's mouth could open so wide (*laughing*). She stopped to catch her breath. Finally!

We created signs for her to do. One blink meant '*yes,*' and two blinks or a stare meant '*no.*' I would say to her "*Mom stop yelling at me just tell me what's wrong so I can fix it!*" But of course, she couldn't talk! I started crying while I was talking to her, and you have to go down the list of asking a question. Like... "*Are your ears itching,*" or "*is your nose itching, do you want to be turned to your other side or is your butt or vagina itching*" and *so on*. Sometimes my Mom would get these boils on different parts of her body like underneath her breast or her vagina hairline. But once you figured it out, she was fine! This woman would burst out laughing at me and then we would both start laughing. As a family, we took care of my Mother very well. The doctors could not believe how well we cared for her. With the help of the sole caregiver, my wonderful Sister-in-law *Tanesha*, (I love her so much), She didn't have to do any of that, but she did and my little big brother and my Stepdad as well as myself along with a nurse that came for four hours a day. We did it! We never argued about taking care of her either; we might have fussed with each other but not about her.

Six years to the day, my Mother passed away. I left her for 15 minutes. When I came back, I walked towards her, and she looked different! It seemed like the nurses had been rushing to get her together when I walked in. I said to whoever was standing there, "*why does she look like that! What's wrong with her?*" My Mother was dying! I had to watch them work on her doing *C.P.R* and all of that stuff. I was on the floor crawling and yelling, "*you killed my Mother!*" with tears running down my face. That was the worst day of my life!! I had to call my family and try to tell them what happened to my Mother and all I could get out is that Mom is dead! When the doctors were finished trying to revive her, I was able to go and see her. She was lying there so peaceful, no stress on her face... her eyes were still open.

I laid in the bed with her for few moments, crying. I told her she was a wonderful Mother and I loved her. My family made it to the hospital, and when they walked in the room, my brother and I just hugged each other. My Stepdad just fell to his knees saying "*No,*" and *he loves her*. We were all crying. I put my hand over her face and closed her eyes. We all just sat there looking at her. My Sister-in-law said, "*She is with her Daddy now.*"

I had a hard time with my Mother being gone. I started drinking *Cîroc* vodka heavily. I began to notice when I looked in the mirror; my skin looked so wrinkled and old. I knew I had to stop. I kept having dreams of the doctors working on my Mom, reliving the scene over and over again. I would close my eyes to try to go to sleep, and I just get startled and wake up crying every time. So, needless to say, I wasn't sleeping at all. One night, my Mother came to me, in my dreams and she was in her wheelchair, and she had on this red coat and this white winter hat that my Stepdad brought for her. I was crying and asking her was she mad at me for leaving her in the hospital by herself. She blinked twice for '*no.*' she was smiling at me and tears were rolling down her face. I felt like she was telling me that she was happy with how we took care of her and to live my life now and for me to *be happy*. I woke up crying real hard, missing her so much. So I felt stronger and had the courage to carry on. I always say… God is probably thinking, "*This woman is talking my ears off.*"

My History Is Not my Destiny

I have told you these things, so that in me you may have peace. In this world, you will have trouble. But take heart! I have overcome the world.
John 16:33

CHAPTER 11
The Monster

On November 7, 2008, a cold winter day, I was diagnosed with Multiple Sclerosis (M/S). They say traumatic stress brings out all kinds of illnesses. I remember being in two car accidents, one on a Friday morning heading home from work. I was at a damn red light, and this car just hit me from behind, and this chic said she didn't even see me! The other one happened on that Sunday night. My girlfriend, Ruby and I were heading out to the club, driving down Covington Highway in one direction and the other car was coming the other way. All of a sudden I was riding over his twenty-four-inch tire. There were sparks shooting out from under my car, so I had to get control of my vehicle. It was like a fast and furious film! The whole bottom fell out from under my car. Finally, I got control of the car, stopped it, jumped out, and ran down the street towards the other car yelling, *"What in the hell is wrong with your damn driving!"* He was standing there with his hands on his head in shock. I had to be in shock as well to go running down the street. *I can laugh at it now.* I didn't even ask this young man *'was he alright?'* All I kept saying *"What the hell happened... and why did your fucking tire come off your damn car!"* I said it about three times. *"Do you know that the tire could have come flying through the window and killed my friend and me?!"* He said, *"He doesn't know why it happened that he just had it put on that evening."*

At the time, I didn't think about where he had the service done, but I should have because they were "At-fault" and the crazy part of this is… the same tire company had the same problem several years later. It was on the news that '*a car tire flew off a car and hit a walker on the sidewalk.*' I called my Mom, This is of course before her incident), and told her what happened and all she kept saying is… "*The devil is trying to get you!*" I said, "*Mom, I don't want to hear that right at this moment!*"

I remember I was on a cruise with four of my girlfriends in October 2008. My first cruise and my right eye was hurting in the back of my eye. It kept flickering; like a light bulb about to lose power. Kind of like closing and opening your blinds to your window. I told my friends what was going on and they said I better go to the Doctors when we get back home. But I still had a blast on my first cruise. So on that Monday, we arrived back in Atlanta. Tuesday morning, I woke up and could not see out of my right eye! I didn't trip at first, but I kept covering up my left eye with my right hand and kept saying, "*ok ok let's try this again.*" So I covered my right eye… then I screamed for my husband that I could not see out of my right eye. He thought I was playing, and I was like, "*I AM SERIOUS… I FREAKING CANNOT SEE!*" All I saw was black! I was blind in my right eye! But I said the other *f-word*. My husband drove me to an eye clinic in Rockdale, Georgia. I told them what was going…the Doctor looked at my eye and suggested that I needed to get an M.R.I. I asked how much would that cost since I didn't have any health insurance. (I've had about twenty MRI's since then. Gosh!). The Doctor said it would cost around a thousand dollars!!

So my first thought was, '*I am going to Grady Hospital!*' So after a few days passed, I finally took my butt to the hospital. Before I went to the hospital, I read on the internet that I had an eye infection, and all I needed was some eye drops. So again, I checked in at the emergency room and told them my story of how I could not see out of my right eye. I had seen Doctor after Doctor that day. I told the Doctor what I read on the internet, and she just shook her head, "*No,*" with a smirk on her face. I finally was taken up to the eye clinic where I had several tests done and was told what was causing my blindness. It is called, "*Optic Neuritis*" which means inflammation of the nerve which it is dead. It is supposed to be pink, but it is white. The Ophthalmologist also said he believes that I have *Multiple Sclerosis* and "*we need to admit you for more testing to make sure.*" I said, "*admit me for my eye?*"

"I have to go to work," and will come back in a few weeks. Well, so here I am, the last patient in the eye clinic getting ready to be wheeled up to my hospital room! I cannot stand being a patient, but I will visit you in the hospital in a heartbeat.

I was a patient from the third of November until the seventh of November. *Oh, my GOD*!! I never use that name in vain, but Lord knows I wasn't ready for that. But God gives you no more than you can handle. I remember sitting in the waiting room for my M.R.I watching *Barack Obama* being elected as our *44th President*. Still not understanding anything that was going on with me.

The Doctors asked me questions about my past motor skills and about any other physical problems, like walking, weakness, and numbness in my limbs. I look back on those question, yes! And now I knew why I felt like that and did strange things. There are so many symptoms of "M/S," and I had most of them! Now I knew why I was deaf in my left ear for ten years and why I would black out. My left arm felt like it was dangling from my shoulder. My legs, at times, felt heavy like a bag of potatoes. My mind also felt disconnected like the puzzle wasn't fitting right or my face felt like it was twisted on my right side. I have been having symptoms since I was nineteen years old and didn't even know it!

It all began when I first blacked out at my Auntie Karen's house. My Mom's younger sister in Los Angeles, California. I was visiting for a few months (it was during the *Rodney King* riots). I was partying a lot, and we were smoking ALOT of weed. So all I remember was that I had been standing by the television and I just fell out on the living room floor! I came around and was like, *"I am high as hell."* I heard my Auntie call out to me, asking, *"What the hell was that noise?"* I answered, *"I blacked out and fell on the floor"* and she said, *"No more smoking for you for a while, am not going to have your Mom kill me if something happens to you!"*

But years later, I kept blacking out and went to the Doctors a few times. All they said was that my iron level was very low. So I started taking iron pills. One night, in 2006, I was getting up to go to the bathroom and passed out between the bed and TV. My husband woke up to my loud thump with me on the floor. He asked me was I *"alright?"* and I just laid there and laughed it off and said, *"Yes."* Then I got up and went to the bathroom. As I got up from the toilet though and started walking back to my bedroom, I passed out again in the hallway. Right in front of my son's room. My son *Josh* came to his bedroom door peeking at me. I saw the lock on his face. His eyes were so huge. My husband jumped up, *"I am going to call paramedics*"! So when they arrived, they checked me out and pricked my finger. It showed I have low iron, but I didn't take it seriously. I had to go to my son's school the next morning for a Parent-Teacher's Conference, but I had a black eye, a busted lip, of course, I told his teacher what had happened, but of course she thought *Joshua's* Father beat the hell out of me!

A few weeks later, I was at my house in the kitchen, getting my hair braided and I felt that *funny feeling* again. I knew I was about to pass out because I know the feeling when it's going to happen. So I had the young lady to yell for my husband (we were going through a divorce at that time) and tell him to come downstairs and right then, I fell and hit my head against the dishwasher. I know I scared the hell out of the little girl, but I always came too with then a few seconds. My husband called the paramedics again. The young lady had to call her Mom and tell her what had happened (I had an '*In Home*' home daycare at that time, and I kept the young lady's little sister). So the paramedics arrived and again they said my iron was '*very low*' and '*I needed to go to my Primary Doctor and get checked out.*' But we did not have insurance at that time. My husband had just switched jobs and so the family was not covered.

So a few days later, I went to a neighborhood health clinic, and the Doctors gave me some muscle relaxers for my arm because it felt like my left arm was hanging by a thread. I didn't understand why it was doing that. So I was taking them and was just getting high off of them. I remember driving our 2001 green Mitsubishi Gallant on Highway 285 north going to pick up my husband from work. It was about 3:30 a.m. and I felt that dizzy and sick feeling in my stomach. So I rolled down all the windows, moved over to the emergency lane and started crying. I called my husband and told him what was going on… he said for me *"to relax, and do not move until I can drive."* I said once before, *"I am never going to get sick!"* First, I thought… when I first received the news, *"you have Multiple Sclerosis,"* God had just slapped me in my face! I figured I had did something wrong in my past and he is punishing me. But now I know, *"all things happen for a reason."* *"And "never judge a book by its cover. You do not know what and how a person is feeling or what they are going through."*

What is multiple sclerosis? WebMD

MS is an unpredictable, often disabling disease of the central nervous system that disrupts the flow of inflammation within the brain and between the brain and body.

A disease in which the immune system attacks, eats away at the protective covering of nerves called the myelin. I describe it has a tire rubber being worn out and it exposes the nervous system.

MS is a long-lasting disease that can affect your brain, spinal cord, and the optic nerves in your eyes. It can cause problems with your vision, balance, muscle control, and other basic body functions. The effects are often different for everyone who has this disease. This can make it hard for it to send signals to the rest of your body.

Early signs of Multiple Sclerosis – Healthline
- Vision problems
- Tingling and numbness of your limbs
- Acute or chronic pain, and muscle spasms
- Muscle Weakness or fatigue
- Balance problems or dizziness bladder issues
- Sexual dysfunction
- Cognitive problems involving concentration, memory, and problem-solving skills

Other Symptoms
Not everyone will have the same symptoms. Different symptoms can manifest themselves during relapses or attacks.

- Hearing loss
- Seizures
- Uncontrollable shaking
- Breathing problems
- Slurred speech
- Trouble swallowing

Diagnosis

A Doctor most likely; a neurologist will perform several tests

- Neurological exam - your doctor will check for impaired nerve function.
- Eye exam - a series of test to evaluate your vision and check for any eye disease
- Magnetic resonance imaging (MRI) technique that uses a powerful magnetic field and radio waves to create cross-sectional images of the brain and spinal cord
- Spinal tap (also called a lumbar puncture) a test involving a long needle that's inserted into your spine to remove a sample of fluid circulating around your brain and spinal cord

Doctors use these test to look for damage to the central nervous system in two separate areas. They must also determine that at least one month has passed between the episodes that caused damage. These tests are also used to rule out other conditions.

A close look at MS symptoms

MS is a disease with unpredictable symptoms that can vary in intensity. While some people experience severe fatigue and numbness, which causes paralysis, vision loss, and diminished brain function.

MS affects an estimated 2.3 million people worldwide. Women are affected more than twice as often as men, according to the National MS Society. Family history is also a significant risk factor. There are different types of MS, but the one I have been diagnosed with is Relapsing –Remitting MS RRMS Involves clear relapses of disease activity followed by remissions that can last for days or even months. Symptoms are mild or absent during remissions, and there's no disease progression during the remission period. RRMS is a most common form of MS at onset. The other ones are, Primary-Progressive MS, Secondary- Progressive MS, and Progressive-Relapsing MS

I am not a doctor. I am an MS survivor and MS advocate. There are so many types of treatments that offer to help with MS like myself. I have been on four different types of treatments, Avonex, Rebif. Those are injectables, Tecferda is a pill, but now I have found one that is working great for me which is called Tysabri, that is an infusion that I have to be hooked up to an IV for an 1 1/2 once a month.

There is a lot of information and organizations available to help and assist those who need to better understand the disease such as:
- National Multiple Sclerosis Society nationalmssociety.org
- The Multiple Sclerosis Association of America. MSAA mymass.org
- Msonetoone.com (855) 676-6326. There is a nurse on duty 24/7
- MS Connections: www.msconnection.org
- Celebrity Supporters-Look to the Stars www.looktothestars.org

There are also many MS connections on social media like Facebook for example. Atlanta MS connections, MSpals, and We're Not Drunk We Have MS, and so on…

"Just like there's always time for pain, there's always time for healing."

— Jennifer Brown

CHAPTER 12
I Am Still Standing

Gosh, I've been through a lot. *But I am here*! And I am not going anywhere until my heavenly Father calls me home. I am in control of my life and my destiny. I am the only one who can make me happy. Someone can contribute to my happiness. But ultimately, my happiness comes from within.

By writing this book, I have healed tremendously. I am not afraid anymore by how people feel about me writing my '*truth*.' Because it's just that, *my truth*. God has shown me that *I have a bigger purpose in my life and that purpose is to help others who are going through what I survived from*. To let them know that they are not alone anymore.

I read and hear all these stories about a young child being molested or violated by someone, and it hurts my soul. *Enough is enough*! I am dedicating my life to bringing awareness, advocating, and working to eradicate sexual assault.

I am in a better place. I am so happy with how my life turned out. This is my new beginning. I know how to give and receive love. I am so thankful for having my sons' support, and other loved ones that helped me through this. I was once told that I had a heart of ice because I was always about self and my beauty was a curse, but my heart has since *softened*.

I was promiscuous growing up and always dated older men. That's all I knew from being molested, as I stated earlier and out to get all of their money. I wonder how my life would have been if I didn't go through what I did. I guess at this point; it doesn't matter because I believe it was meant for me to go through so I can help others learn how to still stand and have courage! In spite of everything I went through, I do believe our life is already written. This is my destiny! I have learned to become my own boss. It's time to *"Get out of other people heads and get in my own."*

Life has knocked me down a few times. I have seen things that I shouldn't have ever seen, but one thing is for sure... *I always got up!* Like Donnie McClurkin sings in his song, "*We fall down, but we get up!*"

It is ok to have *fear*, but know it is *"false evidence appearing real."* Do not let it control you anymore.

I'm so glad that more people are reporting cases of child molestation and sexual assault. Unlike when I went through it, there are now more support systems. The children are our future. We need to nourish and educate them. A child gains his or her self-awareness by the good values that are taught from someone they trust.

Keep in mind that an abuser can be close loved ones like a Mother, Father, Brother, Aunt, Uncle and even School Teachers. Sadly, even your Pastor or a Neighbor can be the violators. Children make a desperate cry for help but are not heard. Listen and pay attention to their cries for help.

Recovering from my Mother's death, I hear her strong words every day, saying, *"You can do anything you put very mind to. Dream, believe, just do it, and know God got you, my baby girl."*

When I was diagnosed with *Multiple Sclerosis*, I thought my life was over. I was not acting like myself at all. I really felt like a monster! My family and my friends thought I was losing my mind. I had to pull it together and tell myself, *"Meshia you are better than this. Your life is not over. This is just the beginning."*

I might have M/S, but M/S doesn't have me! And I am still standing!

I always say "ride it until the wheels fall off." *Let go and Let God*! What I learned from all of this, is that I am a 'Survivor' and I am a brave and a confident woman. I have gone from victim to a real-life victor!

"And I saw the seven angels who stand before
God, and seven trumpets
were given to them."
Revelation 8:2

Unbroken… I Am still standing

I did not choose to wake up that day
to have my heart shattered
into many pieces
but he told me to come a little closer.

I'm Unbroken… I am still standing.
For someone that I trusted
he took my innocence,
that which I did not give,
I cried a river of tears
because my heart
was filled with fear

I'm Unbroken…I am still standing.
It seemed as though he was crushing me
within,
but God helped me hold on to the end.

I'm Unbroken… I am still standing.

With my trembling heart
I let love bring me through
Today I am healed,
strong and free.
Thank the Lord
I'm Unbroken… and I am still standing
and became a better me!

-*Meshia M. Bean*

meshiambean@gmail.com
www.meshiabean.wixsite.com/unbroken

I AM
I WILL
I DID

Made in the USA
Middletown, DE
09 March 2017